Believing in God is too easy

Philippe Orlando

Copyright © 2011 Philippe Orlando
All rights reserved.
ISBN: **0615439551**
ISBN-13: **978-0615439556**

About the author

Philippe Orlando was born and raised in France where he spent the first 27 years of his life. When he moved to the United States he studied biology, graduating magna cum laude from the University of Massachusetts. He has taught high school biology and French for several years. In 2009, he produced and directed a feature-length film, *Happy Anniversary*. He now lives, writes and participates in the Secular Humanist movement in the Washington, D.C. area.

To all the people who taught me

how to think

Humanist Prayer

There is absolutely no grandeur and no beauty
in being some supernatural creature's project
whether it's a God or some other entity.
Because I know you are an ephemeral being,
and I know you will die,
You are infinitely precious to me.
Why would I show care for You
if I believed You are a soul
that will live forever
watched and loved by a God?
If I see You suffer, I can ignore You if
I believe an all powerful God
is watching out for You!

On the contrary,
because I believe everything
You are and everything You do is temporary
fleeting, fragile and gone forever,
it's precious; You are precious!
You are precious because
You won't be here tomorrow.
Not because You are an immortal soul
that I'll see in heaven.
To believe that you live forever in heaven
after you die does not make your life
or mine precious and special.
Worse.
I think such a fairy tale weakens and negates
the need for love here on earth.
We only have each other to love!
Don't waste our lives with your bad dream!
Please, come back!

Contents

Introduction	1
Why must religion be unquestioningly respected?	7
Are you curious or just scared?	11
I think I know how it started	15
How do we know religions were designed by Man?	21
Religion and fast food, same method	27
The Bible	37
The Ten Commandments	43
Intelligent design?	49
What kind of father is He anyway?	55
God has evolved?	61
You think you live in a world created by a loving God!	65
God doesn't need your love and doesn't love you!	73
God never helped us!	77

Explain Haiti to me!	81
Brain injuries and molecules	87
Why her?	91
Faith	95
Praying	101
Feeling God	105
The New Believer	113
Why don't they believe?	121
Why are you good?	125
So you're attracted to that pretty girl or handsome guy?	129
Can God be mad at you for not believing in Him?	135
Conversation with a Christian	139
Why is religion dangerous?	149
It's a crutch, it's a crutch, it's a crutch!	165
Please come back!	169

Christians the founding fathers? Not so sure!

"In no instance have . . . the churches been guardians of the liberties of the people."

            James Madison

"The way to see by faith is to shut the eye of reason."

            Benjamin Franklin

"Religions are all alike - founded upon fables and mythologies.

            Thomas Jefferson

"History, I believe, furnishes no example of a priest-ridden people maintaining a free civil government."

            Thomas Jefferson

The divinity of Jesus is made a convenient cover for absurdity.

            John Adams

Lighthouses are more helpful than churches.

            Benjamin Franklin

Believing in God
is too easy

Introduction

Ignorance is preferable to error, and he is less remote from the truth who believes nothing, than he who believes what is wrong.... It is always better to have no ideas than false ones; to believe nothing, than to believe what is wrong.

Thomas Jefferson, *Notes On the State of Virginia*, 1782

Many books written in the last ten years aim to show that the idea of a universe created by a God doesn't make sense. *The God Delusion* by Richard Dawkins, and *God is Not Great* by Christopher Hitchens are quite good and do make their case. These books generously reference physics, biology and philosophy to make their points. So there is no sense in my using the same approach as these two highly respected authors. Instead I'm going to ask if it is possible with an average educated intelligence, in all good faith (pun intended), truly and honestly to contemplate our world and be convinced that it was created by an omniscient (all knowing), omnipotent (all powerful), all loving God? In other words, is faith alone enough to "prove" or to believe in the existence of such a creator? I don't need the idea of

God. But maybe there is one. Even though I don't need it and don't like it, I can respect the notion of some remote and distant, certainly uninvolved supreme entity, that might have created the universe - just launched it on its course with the Big Bang and let it run by itself. I have a much bigger problem with people who tell me they believe in some sort of personal God who watches over and cares about mankind and who created a set of rules that must be followed by humanity. This fits the definition of the Abrahamic God embraced by Judaism, Christianity and Islam. It is a childish notion of God elaborated by cultures that still had the root of their thinking in the Bronze Age.

The convinced atheist "knows" there isn't any God. The convinced believer "knows" there is one. I strongly believe there isn't any God behind the origin of our universe. I live as if there was no God at all, certainly not one as described by any of the religions. But if I want to be intellectually honest I must point out that I've used the verb "believe" instead of "know." I strongly believe, beyond any reasonable doubt, that our universe was not created by some entity, certainly not one that loves us. But I don't know for sure. This is why I'm not a believer, and this is also why I'm technically not an atheist. They're both too strongly convinced – they leave no room for healthy doubt. I'm a doubter, maybe a weak one, but still a doubter. As Donald Rumsfeld, whom I don't admire, once said, on a totally different subject: "There are things we know that we know, things we know we don't know, and things we don't know that we don't know." My doubt is not whether the God of

Introduction

Abraham created man in his image. That I know didn't happen. It's clear that we share a common ancestor with all other primates. I'm not foolish enough to refute evolution. Huge areas of human knowledge accumulated in the fields of palaeontology, biology, geology, genetics, neuroscience and embryology can't be discarded for pure convenience. Denying the accomplishments of the brilliant architects of these disciplines would simply be ludicrous and would render me an arrogant idiot. Those are the things we know that we know. The source of my doubt lies much further back than the origin of mankind. It arises from the thing that we know that we don't know. The big question is not how humans happen to exist but what was before the Big Bang? Was there "Something" before the universe came into existence? Here I need to open a parenthesis to mention that the theory of the Big Bang simply can't be doubted by the novice. To doubt a scientific theory you need a couple of tools. First you need to understand what it is that scientists call a theory. What they call a theory is something different from what is in the sentence "I have a theory why his wife left him." What they mean by theory is something that can be verified by observations and experiment and repeated at will. You also need to be familiar with the tools that allowed those scientists to arrive at the theory of the Big Bang. If you are completely clueless why the best physicists believe the Big Bang makes sense, you are simply not equipped to refute what they say. You must, at the very least, know as much as they do. There are overwhelmingly convincing scientific observations that indicate that the Big Bang theory is the most serious possibility of how our universe was created. Anybody who doesn't have a PhD in astrophysics and thinks he knows better than those who have devoted their lives to the subject and who are building on the work of previous geniuses should seriously wonder about his own mental integrity and honesty. This is not an essay about astrophysics, if you want to know more about the subject I invite you to visit the department of astrophysics at UCLA and listen to the experts. You'll have no problem finding the site in a Google search. We know there was some kind of event that we call today the Big Bang, but nobody knows what was before it. Now what if some kind of conscious entity was actually behind the origin of the Big Bang? It's unlikely and that concept does not sit comfortably in my intellect for many reasons. But just because I don't buy it or don't feel the need for such a belief, doesn't mean it should be discarded. I must make all efforts not to discard even hypotheses that fail to seduce me. Contrary to many on both sides who insist that they "know," when I ponder what might have existed before the Big Bang I'll say, along with many worthy scientists, "I don't know." It is really with people who say that they *know* that I have a problem. Particularly with the "knowers" who know a God created the universe. The tools and thinking processes which religious believers use to tell me that they "know" God are deeply flawed in many ways.

You are invited to view this book as a collection of thoughts that anybody could have if he or she took the time to stop, wonder, think and observe the world with the tools that our 21st century culture gave us. An open mind is needed. Narcissism (I'm the child of a God), and self interest (I am a soul that doesn't die) must be repressed.

Why must religion be unquestioningly respected?

Those who can make you believe absurdities can make you commit atrocities.
Voltaire

Religion is the last taboo. We can argue about anything...sex, politics, race but not religion. You can disagree with people as much as you want about their views on government's involvement in our daily life, taxes, welfare, being a Democrat or a Republican, about eating meat, whether gays should be able to marry each other and be in the Military, burning coal, drilling for oil, the pros and cons of communism, even whether or not capitalism might actually be a system on its way out. But religious views are off limits? They must be "respected," which means they can't be questioned in any kind of debate, even if I use the most polite and respectful language to offer criticism. I can make fun of just about anything except religion.
Why is that?

Realize what it is you do when you "attack" religion. Contrary to what it seems, you're actually not attacking somebody's view of how the universe came to exist. In my experience most believers are not that curious about how the universe happened, whether it was produced by the Big Bang, by some God or by the fart of some giant cosmic turtle. As long as they are here, alive and kicking and full of hope, all is well. What you are actually telling them, when you criticize their religion and the existence of their God, is that they will not survive their own death. You are proposing another model in which they die into nothingness at the end of the story. This is simply totally unacceptable to them. The afterlife, their afterlife simply cannot be questioned. Each time I hear scientists talk about God and the universe or the absence of God in the universe, it's always to debate how the universe started. Never to wonder whether or not little me, me, me will survive my own death. Science is motivated by disinterested thought, by curiosity and the search for the most probable hypothesis. The religious mind is interested in not dying and in the survival of the soul. A believer's problem is not so much "no God, no universe" but "no God, no soul, I fade to eternal blackness, end of the party, my party." What you attack when you attack people's God is not a God that created the universe. You attack the God that will give them eternal life. The creation of the universe by God is just icing on the cake, a nice "logical" secondary effect, the killing of two cosmic birds with one stone. What is at the center of religion is really the survival, forever, of the believer. Everything else is accessory and is there because it was kind of tough to ignore. No religion would worship a God who created a universe in which humans did not have a soul that survived death. That's why religion is always off limits. You can argue as much as you want about astrophysics and how the universe came into being. But you simply can't go around telling people, who are convinced or are working very hard to stay convinced, that they don't have a soul that survives death and that they will end. But most of all, you can't tell them that their beautiful child is going to die. You will not be allowed to tell them that the amazing light and joy they see in their children and grand-children's eyes is going to one day be extinguished, forever. That beautiful human being that comes from my flesh and blood and that I love so much is going to go to heaven. It's not negotiable. Touch that and you will be in deep trouble. That's why we can't tell people God doesn't exist. Not because they think the Big Bang theory doesn't make sense.

Are you curious or just scared?

*When we are self-indulgent and uncritical,
when we confuse hopes and facts, we slide into
pseudoscience and superstition.*

                        Carl Sagan, *The Demon-Haunted World*

*If you know in advance what the truth will be,
you will never find it.*

                                    Machette Chute

I'm so naive. For a while I actually thought that we simply didn't agree on how the universe was created. I used to think, well, I believe in the Big Bang theory proven overwhelmingly by science, while "believers" believe some god created the universe. We just have different explanations of why we're here. Why not? I should respect that! Then, I realized that's not what it is. You don't give a damn about how the universe was created. You're not that curious. As a matter of fact you're not curious at all. You believe a God created the universe (in 7 days!) because that's the only option that lets you save yourself in the end.

You don't like the idea of a cosmic explosion because it doesn't allow for your immortality. The Big Bang theory tells you that you're just a bunch of molecules organized into thinking organic matter that will, unfortunately, since it follows the laws of entropy, dissolve into the bigger bubble of the universe and you just hate that, don't you? Let me ask you a question. If God had only created the universe but wouldn't give you eternal life, would you believe in that God? If your answer is yes, you're stating that the theory by which you prefer to explain the existence of the universe is that it was created by a supreme being. I might disagree with you, but if you don't go further than that, I can respect you since I don't detect any self-indulgence or self-interest on your part. I have my theory. You have yours. Vive la différence. If your answer is no, that you could not believe in a creed that did not have an afterlife, then it's about time you look deeper inside yourself for what motivates your belief.

I think I know how it started.

The truth will set you free, but first it will piss you off.
                                                            Gloria Steinem

I've always wondered, "When did humans realize they were mortal?" Were we Australopithecus? Homo erectus? Or did we have to wait until we were fully Homo sapiens? Imagine a small group of early humans. What did they think was happening when one of them was killed by a predator and became "something" that resembled the very same meat they had for dinner last night! What did they feel? Did they consciously tell themselves "we are just mobile meat waiting to be killed by something bigger and stronger; everything is just meat, including us?" What of the other death? The quiet, incomprehensible one. What must they have thought when one of them suddenly entered a state that resembled sleep? The others surely waited and waited for him to wake up so they could move on to the next food source. They shook him but he wouldn't wake up. He was pale and his skin cold. The others didn't have a choice other than to wait. Maybe they decided to carry him to their next campground?

Well, whatever they did, they eventually would have come to the conclusion that this was not normal sleep. It was something seriously different. Not only did he not wake up, but his body was starting to change. When they shook him again, they noticed that he had become rigid. Then, and it must have happened fairly quickly in the heat of the African jungle, he started to decompose. That's when things really became ugly. The sleeper became bad meat full of worms. The sight and smell were so repulsive that they had to move away from him. Little by little he started reminding the group of that antelope that was killed by a lion and whose carcass they'd found recently. Eventually humans realized that, even if they survived accidents and violent deaths, all the people in the group one day would fall asleep and never wake up. They all were destined to become nasty meat. It didn't take them too long to realize that this was going to happen to them personally, each and every individual in the group. That is the beauty of becoming human. We are able to transpose onto ourselves what we see happening to others. We're all going to end up like that! You! Me! All of us! Can you imagine what must have gone on in the minds of those first humans? What did they make of this? How, at the dawn of mankind, could you live your life knowing that you're going to become a piece of decomposed meat? We're talking about a time long before any civilization or culture had appeared. We're talking about humans who were barely humans just a few generations before. There was no culture, no philosophy, and no 12 step program to help you, nothing! Just you, the lions and the worms. Nothing to get comfort from(except other meat). So what did we do not to go insane? When we were a different species, a lower primate, we were fine because we were never aware that one day we'd die. But along the way, we graduated from being an animal, not knowing, to a human, painfully aware. But those extra cubic centimeters of brainpower we gained during our passage from clueless animal to human were a double-edged sword! A poisoned present some would say. Sure, it allows you to invent tools, to hunt more efficiently, but it also lets you be aware that one day you'll die! How were we going to live knowing that we will become stinky flesh in the African savannah? How do you live with that grim future? I have turned this around and around in my mind, and I don't see any other way for those early humans, but to invent a part of them, the "soul", that the maggots can't get to. This is the key to sanity. You and your loved ones have a spirit that leaves the body and escapes all the ugliness of putrefaction and goes on forever. You will be, with all the members of your tribe, moved to another world and you will live forever and ever in a utopian "heaven" where no lion can get you! Once we introduce this handy little invention into the picture, life becomes bearable again for the big human brain. An immortal soul that rises out of the rot to live forever has been created. My problem is that I still see the crutch. Today it's not in wood any more, it has evolved, it's more high-tech than the original one, but it's still a crutch. I just cannot buy into the soul concept and neither can our best scientists in neurology. I'll be fine. I'll deal with my own mortality. Being dead is nothing. It's just like not being born. It's that simple. As Mark Twain simply said, "I do not fear death. I had been dead for billions and billions of years before I was born, and had not suffered the slightest inconvenience from it."

How do we know religions were designed by Man?

Writing science fiction for about a penny a word is no way to make a living. If you really want to make a million, the quickest way is to start your own religion.

L. Ron Hubbard (science-fiction writer and founder of Scientology) as quoted in *L. Ron Hubbard* by Bert Corydon and L. Ron Hubbard, Jr.

We are very lucky in this country to have Mormonism as an example. It is so relatively young that it can be historically documented with precision. There are strong reasons to believe that other religions started like Mormonism did. It was "founded" by a hallucinating con artist named Joseph Smith. *The Book of Mormon*, published by Smith in 1830, contains so much nonsense that it should be embarrassing to be a Mormon today. The list of ridiculous claims is long, starting with Smith's claim that he translated it by gazing through magic stones at golden plates shown to him by an angel (he was never able to produce the plates...or the stones...or the angel). Mormons believe that the Native Americans are descendants of an Israeli tribe called Lamanites. They also believe the pigmentation of black people's skin is due to some Biblical curse. They eventually dropped this creed because it was untenable. Still it was in the original book and it is a "fact" that supposedly was communicated by the angel! We know today that being black is the original state of human skin and the only one that can afford protection against ultra violet radiation in Tropical Africa, the original home of humans. Everything other than black is a mutation that happened to the primal black skin. White and other shades of skin colors are just adaptations to different environments. White skin is mainly a way for humans to be able to synthesize vitamin D in the absence of tropical sun light, as in Europe. The dark skin of Africans, who were the ancestors to all modern humans, didn't let them synthesize vitamin D where the sun is weak, like in northern latitudes where humans eventually migrated. The humans who left Africa and moved to Europe gradually mutated to lighter skin shades to be able to make vitamin D under a weaker sun.

Modern genetics have clearly shown that Native Americans came from Asia through the Bering Strait about 15,000 years ago. Of course Smith formulated his crazy ideas before genetics could tell us what we know today. Genetics notwithstanding, it doesn't take a genius to see that Native Americans do look like their Asian counterparts and not like people from the Middle East. Additionally, there is absolutely no linguistic connection

How do we know religions were designed by Man? 23

between any Native American language and Near Eastern Languages. Cows, oxen, asses, horses and goats are mentioned in the book of Mormon as being already on the American continent in 600 BC. We know with certainty that these animals were not present in the Americas until European colonists brought them. Elephants and bees are also mentioned. Mastodons, which resemble elephants, existed in the Americas but became extinct before humans arrived on the continent. As for bees, we know they were introduced by the Spanish. The bees found in America today are still called European bees. The Book of Mormon was obviously written by a man who made it up and didn't know much about the continent on which he was living. Smith couldn't know about genetics, of course, but he was not even educated enough to have read, (and the knowledge was available at that time) that bees had been imported by Europeans. The list of nonsense in the Mormon religion is endless and yet it caught on as a religion in the 19th century, a hundred years after the Enlightenment and despite the fact that science was already able to refute some of its premises. So, if a religion as wacky as the Mormon one could have come into existence in the 19th century and grown strong in the 20th and today, what does it tell us about the other world religions? If a treasure-hunter named Joseph Smith was able, in the middle of the 19th century, to push upon people something he had fabricated, don't you think that somebody in the first century of our era could have done the same? Do you think that people who lived 2000 years ago in the Middle

East were any better armed to resist con-artists and raving lunatics than Americans in the 19th century? How do you know that at the origin of each "great" religion there isn't a Joseph Smith (or several) - just full of bull?

Another very troubling trend is the way religions change. Have you noticed that each time there is a big change in religion it's always made by men? There's never a message from God, whether or not it's through the intermediary of an angel. It's always a group of men who decide that the religion of their fathers is not suited to them anymore so they change it to make their life more pleasant or interesting. When Martin Luther reformed the Christian religion by starting the Protestant Reformation, he didn't do it because he received a message from God. He actually never claimed that he received his insights from some kind of divine word. He did it because he wanted to and he thought it made sense. He introduced concepts such as the one that salvation does not come from good work but is a gift from God, which gave birth to the very disturbing theory of predestination, which basically renders human life as worthless and pointless as that of a rag doll. All these changes came into existence totally arbitrarily because somebody, in this particular case a theologian named Martin Luther who lived in the 15th century, thought it logical. "Sacred texts", followed for generations as the literal Words of God, have in fact been written and then changed multiple times by men (and I do specifically mean men) to suit their own agendas and convenience. If any subsequent modifications are made by

How do we know religions were designed by Man?

men, without any interference from God and are still seen as original, I don't see why I shouldn't believe that the original so-called "sacred texts" were not entirely written (read "invented") by men as well. The propensity by humans to modify the "words of God" at will, should tip anybody off about the flimsy, whimsical lightness of the whole religious precept. It is painfully clear that all the sacred texts found in many cultures have been written by men at a certain time and that they are modified by other men in subsequent times. Anybody who can't see that, and instead sees God talking to mankind, is seriously deluded.

Religion and fast food, same method

Can we be quite certain that it is not precisely religious education which bears a large share of the blame for this relative atrophy [of the intellect of the developing child]? ... By the time the child's intellect awakens, the doctrines of religion have already become unassailable.

Sigmund Freud, *Future of an Illusion*

Considering the crazy precepts of religion and the fact that it asks the individual to shut off his or her brain and accept facts that can't be verified; and because it is so centered on self interest (I am a soul that doesn't die and will go to heaven), can it really capture the minds of fully grown and educated adults in industrialized nations? In other words, is it possible to become religious after having been exposed to physics, philosophy, evolution, and, in general, a solid schooling in the art of critical thinking? A small percentage of people are, after studying these disciplines, still captivated by religion and its promises, but that is a minority. The majority of people who are exposed first to scientific learning (or to science and religion concurrently) do not adopt religion. If anything they might end up believing in something very vague and nebulous, but they rarely end up buying into anything that can be read in the Bible, the Torah and the Koran.

Religion is like junk food. It must hook you while you are young, unformed and ignorant; in short, an intellectual virgin whose brain is very much a *tabula rasa*. No one who grows up in India, Japan or France, raised on the delectable cooking cultures of these countries, can fall for McDonald's "food." By the time you've savored palak paneer, sushi or sole meunière, it's basically impossible to be seduced by Burger King on a regular basis, if at all. Fast food chains know that, and so do religious leaders. That's why they both target children so rabidly. They know if they wait for education to shape the brain first, it will leave very little room for religion and other mumbo-jumbo practices.

Religion, like fast food, must claim the individual before education and critical thinking wire the brain. This is really what it is about, wiring the brain. We are not unconditionally free thinking creatures. We can be modeled into being and believing a certain way. The younger it starts, the more efficient is the wiring. The first wiring pattern will always be the strongest, especially if emotions are also involved. Such is assuredly the case with religion. Depending on what we are exposed to in our childhood, it can be very hard to build other neural paths in the brain. This is exactly why it is so hard to alter religious convictions if they "got you" at the age of five, and you were never exposed to any competing systems while growing up.

Religion and fast food, same method

There is a big difference between what happens in the organization of the brain when exposed to the dogma of religion vs. the intellectual stimulus of true education. With education there is no particular wiring geared toward a set of beliefs. What happens is that the brain is rendered capable of grasping the widest range of possibilities. Education is really the acquisition by the young brain of the best set of tools available at a particular time. Religious education is at the other end of the wiring spectrum. Instead of giving tools to know the world according to investigation, observation and thinking, it imposes an end product and completely skips the processes that lead to that end product. God exists. Period. There's no precise pathway of reasoning to get to that point. It's really just a massive surmise based on wishful thinking. A hoax really. It's a postulate without foundation.

Could this way of thinking have contaminated the way most Americans think? And what if it would explain, partly, the disparity we see between the US and Europe? In Europe any imprint from religion on young minds is heavily counteracted by public education. My family chose to raise me as a Catholic. I was exposed to catechism from the age of 7 to 12. But at the same time, in the strongly secular public French school, secular teachers were giving me, through history, science and philosophy, the tools to put all that religious teaching in perspective. Never were we kids exposed to the crazy notion that "Evolution is just a theory." Never was the proven validity of Evolution questioned. Never did we see, as I saw when I taught biology in the US, a sticker on the inside cover of a biology text book warning students that "Evolution is just a theory as valid as anything else" (read "as valid as intelligent design," which is creationism trying to pass for science).

Definitely the most remarkable tool in my European high school education was the subject of philosophy. Training in philosophy renders the mind extremely inquisitive. Could it be that, among other factors, this might explain why Europe's population is 40% atheist while the US is 10% at best? France has true separation of church and state. The US only pretends to. Do we really have true separation of church and state when nearly every child until the age of 18 has to hear (and say) every day a nationalistic pledge with "one nation under God" in it? Do we even have separation in society at large with "In God we Trust" written on all our currency? Anybody born in the Forties and after has had to go through listening to that polluted pledge. I've taught on and off for about 10 years in public schools in the US. Never have I seen religious precepts and ideas challenged by teachers and institutions. Supposedly in America, all ideas, including false ones, even ridiculous ones, must be "respected."

In the US, I will say without hesitation, we do not teach young people how to think. Instead we teach them how to use their brain within very limited spheres. All the focus is on solving problems of a practical order and examining social issues that have been previously tackled by exceptional individuals. We are very good at this practical form of thinking. But we do not teach children how to think or how to doubt. The big theoretical concepts and the big questions that have been in the back of mankind's mind since the beginning are never tackled, never approached. Is one truly educated if one is never encouraged to debate systems of thought, ethics and religion that were established hundreds of years ago?

It is with the warm nostalgia of someone who didn't know what he had at the time he had it that I look back at some of the heated discussions we used to have in philosophy class about our universe, the nature of Man, and the existence or non existence of God. In America today, in our public schools, not only is it seen as politically incorrect to challenge religion and expose students to alternative views of the world, it's strongly frowned upon. It's actually discouraged to push thinking too far outside the solving of equations and other practical problems. Only a few, who have had the chance to go to some of our best private institutions and to grow up in the right familial environment, have been able to challenge the edicts of priests, rabbis and imams.

Trinity College, in Hartford, Connecticut, is home to the American Religious Identification Survey (ARIS 2008). The last study, done in 2008, tells us that the Jewish population is further ahead in the process of secularization than Americans in general and that African Americans, particularly African American women, are at the opposite end of the spectrum. More precisely, Jewish men have the highest proportion of atheists/agnostics and African American women the lowest. Is that really surprising?

Jewish people are among the best educated in our nation, while sadly our social system has not helped African Americans to access quality education. I've met a few African American women who have been able to disengage themselves from the confines of religion within their culture. Huge credit should be given to these individuals.

There is no such thing as a Catholic, Muslim or Mormon child. Nobody is born carrying such ideologies. There is no ID tattooed on the newborn in the birth canal. Furthermore, nobody becomes Islamic or Catholic or Jewish by just thinking. People "become" one of the above because these ideologies are crammed into young minds and keep any competing ideas from taking over while the young brain is being formed. Neuroscientists know today that the brain will conform and adapt to whatever stimuli it is subjected to. The wiring of the brain by religious teaching restrains further wiring by education. In this respect religious education is actually a form of child abuse. As a result of it, a child doesn't choose who she wants to be, but who her parents want her to be. The best parents would want their child to have the most sophisticated tools to decide what she wants to "know" or "believe" while choosing among all the possibilities available to her. Religious parents just decide for their offspring that there is only one possibility, the one taught by their religion. Daddy is a Muslim, you will be a Muslim. Mommy is Mormon, you will be Mormon. If this is not the best way to limit a child's horizon I wonder what is! Education gives tools, thinking tools to children so they can decide, armed with critical thinking and the best knowledge available to the society of their time, which system of thought, which ideology they'd like to subscribe to. Most of all, the best education allows the young mind, and later the adult mind, to evolve and change according to the evolution of the tools of their society. The world view of the educated mind will change as the person becomes aware of new discoveries in physics, biology and other fields of human knowledge. Real education allows for changes and open mindedness. Religious education ossifies the mind into one way of thinking from which the psyche can't escape. Religious education demands that young people believe that certain myths are true facts, not to be questioned. The world was created by a God. We are souls put by this God into bodies made in his image. He put us on earth to have us go through a series of ordeals so at the end these souls can either go to heaven or hell. This is the way it is. Do not question. Do not doubt. Do not talk back. Religious leaders provide no intellectual tools to apprehend this, but we must believe it without questioning it. We must believe it because it's The Truth. It's not negotiable. This thought process has absolutely nothing to do with the intellectual prowess that built Western Culture. It doesn't form beautiful minds. It molds slavish and sheep-like minds that will let their owners drown in conformism all their life.

Is it pure coincidence that American citizens, who are the most religious in the industrialized world, are also the most apathetic as far as changing and influencing their society or fighting for their rights? I don't suggest we should be like the French, always protesting even when it doesn't make sense to do so. But when was the last time you saw massive numbers of the American people in the streets, demanding that their rights be respected and their living conditions improved? Even the Civil Rights movement doesn't fall into this category. It was motivated by extreme circumstances, undertaken by a small minority of intensely oppressed Americans, mainly Black, who were literally fighting for their freedom and equality. But when was the last time you saw Americans walk the streets en masse - all races, parties and religions together to demand that, like every other industrialized nation, we have a decent health care system, mandatory paid vacation, mandatory paid maternity leave and a decent retirement system? When was the last time you saw an entire segment of American workers walk off the job for even a day to protest wages taxed to pay for illegal and immoral wars?

Could it be that accepting what you have in this world (or in this case what you don't have) is influenced by the kind of education you received and the belief you were forced to swallow as a child that it is all part of some Big Design, predestined by an all-powerful, unchallengeable God? Is the fatalism of Americans a byproduct of their religiosity and a lack of critical thinking in the average American education?

The Bible

The Bible is a wonderful source of inspiration for those who do not understand it.

George Santayana

*You believe in a book that has talking animals, wizards, witches, demons, sticks turning into snakes, burning bushes, food falling from the sky, people walking on water, and all sorts of magical, absurd and primitive stories and you say that **we** are the ones that need help?*

Mark Twain

The fact that nearly all Christians believe the collection of texts we call the Bible is actually The Word of God to men is disturbing. It seems to me that a lot of believers, because they do not feel the presence or their God, just cling to the Bible as the ultimate proof of the existence of their God. "It's in the Bible" is constantly used by believers who really think that it's the ultimate argument that will end all discussions and make them right and you wrong. The origin of the Bible is doubted by generations of brilliant and respected scholars. It has suffered untold numbers of translations, modifications and annotations in two millennia. Modern archaeologists, among them two famous scholars from Israel, Neil Asher Silberman and Israel Finkelstein showed in their book, *The Bible Unearthed*, that the Bible is just a huge piece of entertaining, but utterly unreliable literature as far as history is concerned. The list of mistakes, historical incoherence, and false facts is long.

A small sampling:

Historians and archaeologists have found clear evidence that the Old Testament, which was supposedly written around 3000 years BC, was actually written by people who lived 2000 years after that! Yet they wrote as if they were contemporaries.

There is no trace of Jericho's wall. That city never existed, not as it is described in the Bible. There is no trace of the Exodus – not one shred of evidence that two million people wandered for 40 years in the desert. You'd think they might have left behind a clay pot or two. There is no record from any independent source (including from the Egyptian Empire, famous for its record keeping) mentioning that the Israelis were in fact ever slaves in Egypt. According to the Bible they were and they supposedly escaped an overwhelming army and went to what is today called Palestine. Another piece of storytelling. Leaving Egypt to seek refuge in Palestine could be compared to somebody leaving California to hide in Illinois thinking they had left the United States. At that time,

Palestine was part of the Egyptian Empire! If they had been slaves in Egypt they would still have been slaves in Palestine. In the Old Testament, the use of camels is mentioned during the time of Abraham. It's a known fact that camels were first introduced in the area and used by ancient Israelis at least 1500 years after the time Abraham is supposed to have lived. Hence the hint that the people who wrote the ancient testament wrote it not as contemporaries but more than a thousand years later. The writers had camels and assumed their ancestors must have had camels, too. They were wrong.

The Bible is not even accurate in keeping track of the customs and ways of transportation people used to have. Why should it be trusted for anything else? The mere fact that anybody would surrender his life to the guidance of a text written such a long time ago and so altered over time is mind boggling. To believe in God, is one thing. To believe that the sacred Word of God is contained in a collection of ramblings, in multiple languages, over thousands of years, from hundreds of writers with different agendas which somebody eventually slapped together and called The Bible is truly mind numbing. Certainly, considering the more than 2000 years that separate us from the hypothetical source and the fact that there are only copies of the original text! To illustrate the unreliability of trusting such an old and convoluted document, I'll mention Richard Langworth, who wrote a book called *Churchill by Himself: The Definitive Collection of Quotations*. In it he proves that many quotes attributed to Churchill were in fact never uttered by the famous British leader. We had to await the work of a scholar like Langworth to actually find out about this. So we know we can be wrong about the words of a contemporary leader, a man who was alive when many people reading this were alive, a man who lived when radio and recorded speech were around, a man who was alive until 1955, which is ten years after TV was invented, a man whose language was English! But today, hundreds of millions of people are ready to base their lives on a text written 2000 years ago, the original of which has never been in anyone's possession. The human mind is amazing in its desperation and in its ability to delude itself. The fact that there is also an *Authorized Version* by a King of England doesn't seem to bother too many people. What does it mean if there is a version of anything authorized by a king or a politician? Could it mean that somebody went through previous texts and modified them according to their will and political need? Christians mention the name *The Authorized King James Version of the Bible* without flinching a bit! What if I told you there was a new document we all must live by called "The Authorized George Bush Version of the Constitution of the United States?" Would you follow that book? Would you look desperately for the unauthorized version?

The Ten Commandments

All religions are founded on the fear of the many and the cleverness of the few.

Stendhal

I like the Ten Commandments. I really do. I can imagine how something similar might have been created by a small group of people. A long time ago, when we were barely starting to get organized in society, a group of older men and women (at that time, people in their mid-30s, maybe mid-40s) gathered one day to find a solution to something that had been plaguing the early human societies from the beginning. Something that they thought was going to keep humans from really moving forward. Many times they had tried to find a solution to this particular problem, but in vain. What problem are we talking about? Something carried over from our primate past. Something also shared by our closest animal relative, the chimpanzee. Young males were constantly going on rampages and killing, killing, killing. They killed other males to have access to females. They killed females who don't want to have sex with them. They wanted something, they killed and took it. All that killing was like a cancer eating the early human societies. Life had been good. People had learned how to cultivate the land, and they didn't have to hunt animals to eat anymore. They raised cattle. They lived in a fertile land where everything was plentiful. Still young males coming from other groups of humans killed a huge number of their humans. They'd tried everything. Nothing worked. The young brutes just didn't see what they had to gain by not killing. Imagine this scenario: an older, wiser woman confronts a group of young thugs and tells them "If you keep killing like that you're....I'm going to...." She stops. First she stops talking because she just can't find anything to say. What was she going to say anyway? "If you keep killing like that I'm going to...do what?" "If you don't stop killing, "something" is going to happen to you?" And what would that be? She knows there is nothing she can threaten them with. Absolutely nothing is going to happen to them if they don't stop killing! Eventually she stops talking because they kill her. Of course, why not? They steal all she has. They rape her daughters and kill one because she is not cooperating. Then they depart, leaving behind them a totally devastated group of older people and kids. One more time the group of elders gathers to find a solution. Again they agree that there is nothing they

could do or tell those killers to keep them from killing us. Finally one of them says "I think I have an idea. We need the help of something bigger. I've noticed that even though they kill, they're terrified by death. Like the rest of us they believe they have a soul that keeps on after their bodies die. We need to tell them that the Being that created the world has also given us a set of rules and we're only going to live after our death in another world if we follow those rules. They don't fear us, but they do want to keep living in an after world after they die. We must convince them that one of us got the message from the Creator, a set of rules that must be obeyed." They all agreed that it was the best thing they had come up with. They decided that by morning they must have agreed on a set of rules. They realized that they had to be smart, and that some embellishment of these rules should be made. The young killers must really think the rules came from the Creator of the world. So in addition to the rules against killing, there must be other rules that would establish God's power. It was decided that the rules, since they were coming from God, would be called Commandments, which would give them a non-negotiable aspect. Since they seem to have no respect for older people we should have something like this:
"Honor your father and your mother, so that your days may be long upon the land which the Lord your God is giving you." Somebody proposed the idea: "You shall not kill." To keep them from having sex with women who belong to other men they came up with: "You shall not

commit adultery." So they don't take all our stuff we should have: "You shall not steal." We could reinforce it with: "You shall not covet your neighbor's house; you shall not covet your neighbor's wife, nor his manservant, nor his maidservant, nor his ox, nor his donkey, nor anything that is your neighbor's." And then to make it all scary enough to have the desired effect, they added the first four commandments which all demand total obeisance to a powerful God.

That's how I believe it all started. The Ten Commandments and similar rules originated in an attempt to keep groups of young males from murdering the rest of us when they wanted properties and women. Still today, the people among us who continue killing us, robbing our possessions, raping our women and molesting our children are young males. They are also the most likely to be convinced to go to war for no good reason. If it's such a huge problem today, just imagine what it was like 10,000 years ago.

Intelligent design?

Science is open to criticism, which is the opposite of religion. Science begs you to prove it wrong - that's the whole concept - whereas religion condemns you if you try to prove it wrong. It tells you to accept it on faith and shut the hell up.

Jason Stock

Scientific beliefs are supported by evidence, and they get results. Myths and faiths are not and do not.

Richard Dawkins

The molecule that transports oxygen in the blood of all mammals, birds, reptiles, most fish and many other creatures is called hemoglobin. It picks up oxygen in the lungs and becomes oxyhemoglobin when a molecule of oxygen binds to a particular site on it. When oxyhemoglobin arrives in cells, the molecules of oxygen are released within the cells to take part in cellular respiration. This mechanism looks so perfect that many might see the "intelligent design" of a divine creator behind it. Nope. Not even close. If there is any intelligence behind the construction of hemoglobin, it's a malicious one. If benevolent, good-intentioned intelligence had been involved, the molecule of hemoglobin would have been created by God to carry life-giving oxygen only. Unfortunately hemoglobin's binding affinity for carbon monoxide (CO) is 200 times greater than its affinity for oxygen. That's right. In the presence of both oxygen and carbon monoxide, hemoglobin will choose carbon monoxide, and you will die. That's what happens to people who find themselves in a room where the deadly product of carbon combustion is released from a leaky heating device burning coal, oil or gas. These people die because the hemoglobin in their blood picks up molecules of CO instead of oxygen. Very quickly all the hemoglobin is taken up by CO and there's no free hemoglobin to carry oxygen to the cells anymore. The affinity of hemoglobin for CO is so great that the two never separate. That's why people who are poisoned by carbon monoxide can't be saved by resuscitation techniques, or by bringing them outside in an attempt to expose them to fresh air. The only thing that can save them is a blood transfusion, bringing new hemoglobin to their system.

Question to believers and tenants of intelligent design:

Why would God have created hemoglobin with a greater affinity for carbon monoxide than for oxygen?

Intelligent design?

If hemoglobin had really been created to carry oxygen to our cells by a loving Supreme Being it would not carry anything else. The notion of intelligent design would require that something as vital as the molecule that carries oxygen to our cells would be perfectly designed. It's not.

Answer from Evolution:

The hemoglobin molecule didn't evolve in humans. It was carried over from previous creatures, way up across the mammalian line and from the fish one. Probably even before. Earthly creatures never had to evolve in the presence of fossil fuel combustion in stoves or cars or other human systems. Before humans started to use heating systems, hemoglobin never had to choose between picking up oxygen or carbon monoxide. Nature never had to choose something other than hemoglobin to carry oxygen to cells because there was never any other gas competing with it. It's only when man started to live in closed environments and needed to heat them that he ran into a problem. This is consistent with the mechanism of evolution. Hemoglobin worked perfectly in the natural world and it stayed the way it is today because its greater ability to pick up CO over oxygen was never a problem, since there was never CO around in any significant amount to be a problem. An omniscient God would have known that one day his favorite creature, Man, would use fossil fuels and might die from using them. An intelligent, caring, loving God would never have created his children with a blood that has an affinity for anything other than the vital molecule of oxygen. A loving heavenly Father would have known and planned better.

What kind of father is He anyway?

To err is human. To torture your children for an eternity is divine.

John Quinley

Raccoons, rats, sharks and flat worms find their food in nature. All they have to do is find it and take it. Most of them succeed, since as far as I know those species have existed for millions of years and are still with us today. So it's fair to say that a large number of raccoons, rats, sharks and flat worms find food everyday and are able to survive and reproduce without saying thank-you-God before each meal! I, a human, on the other hand, am supposed to have totally different deal. I'm the prodigal son. I'm God's favorite creature; so favorite that he made me in his image. Don't you think this would give me a more favored position among other earthly creatures an allow me to behave accordingly in my daily routine? A rat can just dive into a dumpster and gorge and skulk away happy. But I'm supposed to anoint myself in thank-you each time before I put food in my mouth. Worms and rats don't have to be grateful for their meals, but I, a human, God's favorite pet, I'm supposed to lower my head and praise him each time I eat. Thank you master, yes master! The preferred son has reverently to pronounce his gratitude to the father each time he eats - while creatures that live in sewers and give the preferred son diseases like the Plague don't have to "behave" or be grateful for anything. Sorry but I'm missing something here. If I'm truly his most beloved creature, why do I have to pay my respects and show my gratitude for something a rat can have for free? God appears to be a father who cares more about the neighbor's kids, the rats, than his own kids, the humans. Why did my Father create a bacterium that can kill me, his favorite creature? A microscopic unicellular organism with no nervous system, no free will, and no self-awareness. It can kill me in horrible pain. Why? By the way, according to most believers I've talked to, I'm supposed to feel bad for asking such questions? I should simply resign myself to the fact that I can't figure this one out! What did I do to deserve to become weaker and weaker and plagued with diseases, as I get older? Is this a way to treat your favorite son? All the parents I know want the best for their kids, but our Father in Heaven seems only preoccupied with showing us how weak, miserable, vulnerable and mortal we are, and how powerful He is. We are supposed to love him unconditionally but all we get in return is cancer, shot knees, hip replacements, loss of vision and lower back pain.

Next to what God has had in store for us humans throughout the ages, *Les Misérables* looks like an uplifting story. I haven't killed anybody. I haven't robbed anybody. Frankly, I haven't created too much disturbance for my fellow human beings. So basically all my mistakes are small stuff and look how he can punish me! With carcinomas, rotting bones, blindness, even worse, baldness! On top of the many joys of aging, two-thirds of mankind, roughly four billion people are not eating properly and a good one billion are living in abject poverty and they have done nothing! They have done nothing to deserve their fate and I have done nothing to deserve my life of relative plenty. Just pure luck. I was born in the Western Hemisphere with an average intelligence; they were born in places like Bangladesh. Some of those unfortunates are twice as smart as I am and would achieve far more than I in my privileged environment - but God has decided they won't make it. It's time for our little refrain: "God works in mysterious ways!" I mentioned a bacterium with no free will or freedom. Well I don't have freedom either. I would love to be able to stand tall on this planet, but I'm not permitted to. Believers tell me this is not my project. I'm not even my own project. Can you believe this? Believers believe I'm God's project. According to any religion you could name, He (it's always a he) didn't create me as a free being in control of my own destiny, belonging to myself and making my own rules. He created me so HE could give me two choices: Heaven or Hell, and rules to follow. I myself would give more choice to any drug-addicted kid under my care and responsibility in a halfway house. But what do I know? If I'm his favorite kid, God should be reported for child abuse. Any parent who would treat his kids the way He does would be in serious trouble in any human society. I don't need, I don't want; I don't care about such a father. As far as I'm concerned He can go to hell!

God has evolved?

Have you noticed how believers insist on the fact that God has changed since the *Old Testament*? Supposedly the God from the *New Testament* is kinder, better, more loving than the one from the *Old Testament*. They really insist on this. I understand their embarrassment, but there is absolutely no message from God, no sacred text, no nothing that has been found engraved on some stone in some cave or delivered on some hill by an angel that tells us that God has softened his touch since the *Old Testament*. This is simply not in the Christian mythology and folklore. The God from the *New Testament* is the same jealous, bloody psychopath described in the *Old Testament*. It's only some slightly embarrassed believers who feel the need to modify the angry, psychotic God of the *Old Testament* when they realize they'd look like fools to actually venerate such a supreme being. I detect the same embarrassment when Christians try to tell us that they actually believe in evolution, that the concept of God is not incompatible with evolution. I beg to differ. The process of evolution is not what an all powerful, all knowing God would use for life on earth. Evolution is messy, random and shouts trial and error - not the work of a supreme God who knows what he's doing. Why would God build gills and a tail on a human embryo (yes, they're there-look it up!) only to destroy them later in gestation, before anybody witnessing a birth can see them? Why would God waste time building structures during the first 4 weeks of pregnancy and then remove them? Do you realize what a wasteful process it is for a developing embryo to mobilize protein, calcium and calories to build a tail and gills that will eventually be destroyed later in fetal development? Why wouldn't an all-powerful God make humans the way they are from the first moment of conception - the way they will look at birth? An all-powerful God could certainly do that! Why would a perfect god cause embryos to develop as if their ancestors had come from fish and passed through creatures that had tails? Of course when you point that out to believers they always have the same answer: "God's ways are unknowable!" It is intensely irritating when religious people try to get away with such little semantic tricks. Some go even further. The gills and tail in the human embryo are actually evidence planted by the devil. That's what a Christian told me once. There is a battle going on during the development in-uteri between good and evil. The devil always manages to have gills and a tail appear at the same time during pregnancy and, then, God always manages to destroy them. I've always wondered, if God is so all-powerful, how come he doesn't keep the devil from creating those structures in the first place? When I mention to these poor souls that we have actually discovered that it is the same set of genes that makes a tail grow in the embryo of a monkey, a cow, a cat or a human most of them remain speechless. Obviously the devil works in mysterious ways. Humans just have a set of genes that are turned on at a particular stage during pregnancy to make the tail disappear. Animals that are born with tails don't. It's so easy to embarrass believers by pointing out facts and events that have been explained by science. Still you can always trust them to attempt some acrobatic explanation that will always be an insult to your intelligence and an acknowledgment of their ignorance.

You think you live in a world created by a loving God!

The universe we observe has precisely the properties we should expect if there is, at bottom, no design, no purpose, no evil and no good, nothing but blind, pitiless indifference.

                Richard Dawkins, *River Out of Eden,* 1995

Either we are not free and God the all-powerful is responsible for evil. Or we are free and responsible but God is not all-powerful. All the scholastic subtleties have neither added anything to nor subtracted anything from the acuteness of this paradox.

                              Albert Camus

Let's assume there is a "God"-with a capital G. Let's assume that, like any good person of faith, you believe that God created the world and everything in it. Now, take a really good look at the world around you. What does it tell you about your God? Do you truly believe a Supreme Being full of love built it? Look at the way life is organized on this planet. Watch the evening news. Check out the latest offering on Animal Planet. Stop in at the natural history museum. Your loving and compassionate Father cooked up a Garden of Eden based on murder! Let's assume that all the problems with which mankind is plagued with have been brought onto us by our bad behavior in some biblical past. Let's assume we're paying today for something humans did or didn't do in the past. Fine. But what about the rest of creation? What did squirrels, elephants and baby antelopes, (some of them are regularly eaten alive by baboons), do to deserve the multitude of horrible things happening to them? For billions of years before man appeared on this planet, animals have been basically doing the following things:

a) Trying to kill another creature to get the protein in its body.

b) Trying to escape being killed by another creature that considers their body as source of protein.

c) Mate and try to avoid being killed during the reproduction process (fights, sometimes to death, between males to access females; females killed by males during copulation, offspring killed by competing males, etc…)

In all these earthly occupations, the likelihood of dying a painful and violent death is very high!

What a life!

You think you live in a world created by a loving God!

Your loving God one day got up and said to Himself "Let's create life on planet Earth! I'm going to have a world in which creatures will have to spend their lives killing or trying to escape being killed. Oh, and just for fun, let's make sure those brutal deaths are rarely quick and painless. Let's drag them out and crank up the agony-meter. It's going to be a world in which species will be perpetually at war with each other." Think about that. Satan himself could not have conceived of anything worse! Short of a world in which everybody is tied to a stake, and tortured with fire, what's worse than a world perpetually in agonizing war where other species are constantly looking for you, days and nights, to kill you? What's worse than a world in which you need to kill other creatures in order to find nutrients for your body? This is insane! I'm supposed to believe a loving God designed that?

Complex animal life was here hundreds of millions of years before man appeared. For countless eons before we arrived, animals have been murdering each other on this planet with no humans to witness it and derive any kind of "lesson" from it. So the argument that suffering was created to make man think about his morality and his behavior just doesn't hold. If man was not here to learn something from watching dinosaurs kill each other for hundreds of millions of years, then what was the senseless killing for? Was it so these behemoths with brains the size of a kiwi could appreciate life and ponder about it and improve their manners? Enjoy sunsets, maybe?

I also do have a bit of a problem with the mind of an all-knowing, all-powerful Creator being entertained by wormy, invertebrate life at the bottom of the oceans for hundreds of millions of years, then creating only moderately more interesting animal life forms for another few hundreds of millions of years and finally one day saying, "I am so bored. I think I'll whip up something with arms and legs and a heart and a conscience and - guess what.....just for fun, he's going to be so screwed up! He'll be able to love and learn and strive for worth and nobility, but I'll make sure to shower him with disease and agony and war and failure and heartbreak and unbearable loss. Now that should be worth watching for another few million years!" Let's put God's planning process in earthly terms. Imagine a huge lab; say a generous portion of Nevada. We'll give it to brilliant, caring scientists where they can create life from scratch with full control over everything. In that lab, they will be the creating "gods". Do you honestly believe that any of these Nobel Laureates would intentionally shape a world where their creations are going to have to fight, maim and kill each other to stay alive? Only psychos would do that. I think these nice, intelligent people would create a world in which all creatures derive all the nutrients they need from something totally benign -- sunlight perhaps. They won't need predators to control herbivores. The number of creatures would be controlled naturally to avoid overpopulation. They'd have hormones and pheromones to naturally control reproduction when their numbers are above or below a certain threshold. Our new creatures wouldn't be able to reproduce if there were too many of them because of sets of genes that would be turned off and wouldn't drive them to procreate. But they'd still be able to mate, because we'd make mating so good (but most of the time they'd be shooting blanks). Every creature will die naturally of peaceful old age. All powerful gods could create such a world if they wanted to.

That's not the world that your God had in mind for you. You live in a world that a sadistic maniac would have built. A world of perpetual fighting and misery. And what if I don't want to fight and kill? Does that mean I won't develop and thrive...or even survive...because I won't harm my fellow creatures? That sounds to me like the games Nazis used to play with people in concentration camps. You want to stay alive, sure, here's my gun with only one bullet. You can kill yourself or kill either your son or your father. If you kill yourself, both will live. If you kill one of them, you'll live and so will the other one. But you must kill. God also decided that for all creatures, man and beast, life would be short, nasty and brutal. God lovingly deemed that we'll have cancer, and we'll feel horrible pain, both physical and emotional. After the joy of sex, most females will give birth in pain, and to be able to know the joy of sex, males of all species will have to compete against each other to access females. That's right. If you want to mate, you have to first "win out" against your brother. That's still how it works in the animal kingdom and the human system is only a slightly more civilized version. Sometimes a child will be born with some horrible deformity! And sometimes animal mothers will see their babies eaten alive by predators (sometimes males of their own species!) who are actually waiting for the chance! And before we die, all of us in the broad animal kingdom will become old and ugly and very weak. We'll lose our teeth, our eyesight, our mobility, our hearing, and our minds. "Ah, yes," muses our loving God, "it's going to be so entertaining. And, so they can properly thank me for that world of horror I've given them... and to really mess up their brains... I'm going to demand that they love me, and, fools that they are, some actually will!"

I could maybe, in one of my worst, depressed, darkest days, in which my brain lacks sleep, oxygen and nutrients, actually guess at the holy reasoning behind this insanity. Of course! God maybe wants to make a world of ordeal for humans in order to reward them. Sure, why not! Let's make us appreciate life and what we have by making us aware that we will be sick, old, in pain, sightless, etc. (and oh, what a long list it is). But what's the point in having raccoons or lions or ospreys go through the same ordeal? Do you really believe that they'll get a lesson out of that? A lesson that other critters can learn? Do you really believe that a blind opossum is actually learning a lesson from being blind and that he enjoys life more because of that infirmity before being killed by a fox? What exactly is the point of creating elephants that will lose their teeth and take months to starve and be eaten alive by lions as they fall exhausted into the mud? Who's getting a lesson out of this, the lion or the elephant...or the bacteria decomposing the elephant? Finally, what crime did mankind commit in a distant past to deserve such punishment? What did we do? It better be something big, huge! Did we kill another brother species? Did we try to kill God? That's nonsense; we couldn't kill a God! So what did we do to deserve the world we have today? Ah, now I remember. We bit into the forbidden fruit of knowledge. We're actually being punished for wanting to know the nature of our universe. And better yet, we're to blame! By munching into that apple in the Garden of Evil, God draped us in the mantel of Free Will. So now He gets to point the finger at us. "You chose, so it's your fault!" Some educated westerners in industrialized countries are actually getting along with that?

Your God is either incompetent, in which case he wouldn't have been able to create the universe, which means he's a figment of your tired imagination, or if He exists...he's completely psychotic. We'd be better off without HIM.

God doesn't need your love and doesn't love you!

I was told once by a woman that "her God was madly in love with her." What kind of supernatural, omnipotent, all-powerful creature, other than the one living in her imagination, would "fall in love" with her, with humans? That mighty, all-knowing being, which supposedly created the entire known universe with billions of galaxies in it....loves us? That amazing being loves me and needs my love? Me? A human whose body is degenerating by the minute, who has a very narrow and incomplete vision of the universe and who is, by God's standard of time, certainly by the universe's standard of time, going to die soon. What does it mean to believe that we are loved by such a powerful being? Is this the mother of all ego trips? It looks like it. What kind of Supreme Being is that? I mean, frankly, if you need the love of most of the humans I see throughout my day, you're in trouble, whether you're a god or not. If you were God and you were about to create something to love, would you create humans? Why not love another God? Another supreme being that doesn't die? Would you really create little creatures who would live on a crumbling planet; little creatures made of flesh and blood, plagued by diseases? What's the point of being God if you can't create something to love at least half as great as you are? Why create such an imperfect creature, a human, to be the object of your love? I've seen those who prey on the love of "smaller" people. They're usually dangerous psychos. Most of the time, they want to control somebody smaller than they are because they're not able to get the love of their peers. Between me and a god, it simply can't be love among equals. I'm not a god. Love can only work when both parties are more or less equal, in the same league. When it's not the case very bad things happen. It's not love; it's dependence and control. Control, uh? Look at the set of rules God made for us and look at what happens if we don't obey them. By the way, somebody like me, a small and insignificant creature on a small planet would love to be loved by a god. I mean, please sign me up? If somebody way bigger and better than you loves you, it means that you yourself are greater and better than you thought you were… unless something really fishy is going on here! Maybe there are many gods out there and the one who created us and our universe is a loser. He's such a loser that he can't get the love of other gods so he created little humans to love and be loved by? Maybe it's a child god and we're his toys? Here I make rules for them, there I punish them!

God never helped us!

Each time there is improvement in the human condition it's never because of divine intervention. Never. Ever. When a very small number of humans decide to start horror on the planet, God never stops it. Never! When a madman decided to gather 6 million Jews (God's very own Chosen People) into concentration camps and gas them, burn them and make lampshades with their skins, God just watched and did nothing. The horror was stopped by humans-when tens of thousands of American, Russian and British men gave their lives to stop the unspeakable torture. Since the beginning of mankind God has watched the polio virus mutilate countless humans, the majority of them innocent children. Don't you think a loving, caring father would have intervened? Okay, we won't even ask Him to cure all viruses, but maybe He could just pick one, so we know we're not alone! Humans had to wait until the twentieth century to find a cure themselves, without the help of any loving heavenly father. We can say the same any disaster afflicting mankind. Name any disease, natural disaster, war, poverty. Each time a solution is found it's never because God did it. Humans always did.

It would seem reasonable to at least find one instance in which God decided to intervene. Just once in the 2000 years since the supposed visit of his son, Jesus. He could have picked just one thing. He could have chosen the Armenian genocide, or the biggest genocide in modern history, the one of the Native Americans, or the enslavement of Africans in the New World, or the Holocaust, or the killing fields of Cambodia or Rwanda. God didn't seem to believe he had to spare the lives of the 2 million Vietnamese people who were killed by the U.S. for nothing, since Vietnam did eventually become communist. We're not asking to be helped and assisted all the time. Just once. Please, just once. Oh, right. I forgot about free will. We blew it in Eden. We would have been innocents in Paradise, protected from all harm. But then we bit into the fruit of knowledge and God forever cursed us with free will to create an unholy mess of the world. Well that makes sense. After spending a whole day creating these perfect beings, they screw up with one petty violation and their loving father-creator says, that's it! One strike and you're out. From now on, you're on your own. Why can't it be like baseball or California - three strikes and you're out? Not very forgiving, our Father, uh? When you think about it we are actually punished for not remaining stupidly innocent? We are punished for wanting to know more about the world and reality. Are we being punished for discovering the laws of physics that are ruling and ordering our universe?

Explain Haiti to me!

Haiti was populated with slaves brought from Africa. While in slavery these people suffered immensely at the hands of their French captors. Finally, in 1804, they managed to revolt and succeeded in kicking the French off the island. At that time, Napoleon was preparing his invasion of Russia. The number of French forces in the area was small and he didn't have time to focus on Haiti. He proposed a deal to the newly freed people. If you don't want France to come back later with more troops, you must pay reparations. The US at that time was already the main ally of France. Americans were afraid of the example Haiti could set for the southern states as the first nation composed of free slaves. So they helped France enforce the paying of reparations. The amount of money paid was so huge that Haiti was never able to accumulate enough wealth in all its history to replace the lost funds and build a nation. The debt was finally fully paid in 1947. The Haitian people worked for almost 150 years to pay back France. After that they were invaded several times by the US and murderous dictatorships succeeded one after the other. If there are a people who, as a nation, never exploited, invaded or oppressed any other country, it's the Haitian people. If there are a people who suffered hideously from the beginning of their history until today, it's the Haitian people. So when an omnipotent, omniscient, all loving and immensely good and fair God knows that a huge earthquake is going to strike Haiti in January 2010, how come he decides not to intervene? What kinds of lessons are the Haitians supposed to get out of this? Is this endless litany of suffering meant to teach them something in particular? Was this last ordeal perhaps meant to teach a morality lesson, not to Haitians, but to the rest of the world? Really? What kind of God would so severely punish a people who have already suffered so immensely to teach a lesson to other people who haven't suffered as much? And what could the lesson possibly be? Please show me a French, German, Bhutanese or US citizen who actually learned something from what happened to Haiti. Please explain to me how Haitians or the rest of the world were morally elevated when the earth shook on that already mistreated island. Do you remember Pat Robertson, the senile Southern Baptist minister who predicted in 1976 that the world was coming to an end in October of 1982? Did you hear him say that the earthquake was actually God punishing Haiti for their "pact with the Devil?" There is no doubt that Robertson has the I.Q. of a radish, but I can guarantee you that he never believed what he said when he mentioned that pact with the Devil. What happened to Haiti is actually a huge problem, not only for Robertson, but for most religious leaders. How do you explain to your confused flock that a compassionate God full of love let such a horrible thing happen to one of the most distressed nations on earth?

A nation of former slaves who went from one ordeal to another, constantly oppressed and exploited by rich nations? How do you reason this one away and still keep your spiritual composure?

If you're a minister you have basically two choices:

If you are not a great "spiritual" leader, just a small fry-pastor, the easiest way out is to retreat one more time behind the very convenient but unacceptable (to anybody with half a brain) "God works in mysterious ways." If you have a bigger reputation to defend and are watched by millions of believers on the idiot box, you must come up with a better explanation. So... the only reason why a compassionate God full of love would let such a disaster happen to an already oppressed people is to actually punish them for something huge. And it better be huge. What kind of massive offense could these poor people have committed that would explain to distressed and perplexed believers why God actually let this earthquake happen? Obviously when we look at history we find no reason. Nothing can be found in the real physical world. Why not look in the unseen world! In other words in the wild imaginary world of gods and demons. That's it! They made a pact with the Devil to beat the French! Here we go. If you make a pact with the Devil, of course God is going to be mad at you. Not only should he let an earthquake destroy you, but I bet the God described in the Old Testament would actually be capable of causing one. That's why, my dear brothers and sisters, Haiti experienced such a disaster. It was actually God punishing them. Suddenly everything makes sense. At least for people who have shut down their frontal lobes and given up all thinking and who subscribe joyfully to the fairy tale of Christianity. Even Christians should (but let's not assume anything here) think that it's kind of weird and unfair for God to give Haiti an earthquake in 2010 for something they did in 1804. But let's not underestimate the power of the confused mind. I bet myriads of believers are able to find an explanation that satisfies them. On the other hand, anybody with even average intelligence will note that history has shown that nobody has ever needed the help of the Devil to beat the French at war. And if the Devil did help the Haitians, what kind of a good deal exactly did they get from the Devil in return? A debt that took 150 years to pay back? A succession of invasions and dictatorships? Cholera? Of course even the same sub-standard IQ might wonder what kind of God would punish a people for a "sin" committed by their ancestors 200 years ago. You can turn it any way you want in your mind, it will never make sense. Haiti is not the only poor country that is constantly plagued by disasters. Thousands of people die each year in floods in Bangladesh, another country that was created out of the will of a people to be free from oppression when the British Empire left India. When you ask believers how come their God has not extended His loving hand even a fraction of an inch to alleviate some of this agony, all you get is incoherence that makes you wonder how these people function in the modern world. At best what you get is the sorry spectacle of a religiously brainwashed mind reciting its favorite mantra. "God's ways are unknowable! God works in mysterious ways! We're not supposed to know the big plan!"

Everything makes sense, everything is much easier to explain if we agree there is no God watching, certainly not a fair, compassionate, loving one.

Brain injuries and molecules

According to many religions, certainly according to Christians and Muslims and many other creeds, we are souls momentarily inhabiting bodies. When our bodies die, depending on how we've lived, we go to different places, heaven or hell.

How is this belief, this "hypothesis" confirmed by observation? And if it's not, why not? I won't even waste time in any futile attempt to demonstrate whether or not heaven and hell or the soul, for that matter, exist. I just have a few questions. See if you or your spiritual guide can answer them.

When I go to heaven, who am I going to be? The person I was before or after Alzheimer's? Am I going to be the gentle human I used to be or am I going to be the insane person who has lost the ability to tell good from bad because a certain part of his brain was destroyed in a car accident or by a bullet? We've all seen cases (especially of dementia) where someone who used to be intelligent and loving becomes but a shadow of himself, barely able to focus or think straight. What got lost - the brain or the soul? When that person dies, how will she be in heaven? The caring genius she used to be before losing her edge or the wasted, diminished version of herself? If her greatness was in her soul and her soul is HER, then how come she loses it when her brain ages? How come the bigger the brain of animals the bigger their intelligence and personality? We all know that big brained apes, dolphins and dogs have bigger personalities than small brained lizards. Doesn't this point to the fact that brain matter *is* personality? Does my personality reside in the gray matter of my brain or in my soul? If it resides in my soul, why do I have a brain? Why do I need one? I could just function with the structures that control heart beating and breathing and other automatism, but why do I have a neo-cortex for thinking and parts of my brain that control emotions? If who I am, my personality, resides in my soul, how come my personality can be changed and altered by medications, drugs and chemical compounds that affect the brain or by brain injuries? What gets drunk, the brain or the soul? If the drunken brain raped the girl or killed the villagers in Afghanistan, why didn't the soul stop it? Who is depressed and needs Prozac, the brain or the soul? If what we are is ruled by an immaterial "soul", don't you think that molecules, which are actual, material structures that can be seen under a microscope, should not be able to change our mood? If chemically altered molecules can make us happier, what's happier, the brain or the soul? Who are you, a brain or a soul? When you have surgery and you're unconscious because of the molecules of gas the anesthesiologist administered, where's the soul? Who's out, the brain or the soul? If the brain is out, where's the soul while you're having surgery? How come when we shut off your brain with chemicals YOU are not there anymore? Could an immaterial soul be shut off like that? What does all this tell you about the probable residing place of your consciousness and personality? Is it in a material brain or in an immaterial soul? You might say that while we're on earth we are brains and that is what matters. But again, who's going to be rewarded in heaven? The brain that got altered by some chemical or was injured in an accident, leaving you a creature insensitive to the most basic ethical problem, or the soul? We know the brain will decompose, so it can't be rewarded in heaven. Is the soul the one in control then? If the actions of the soul on earth are what matters to determine what kind of reward an individual will get, heaven or hell, then the soul should always be the one in control! Apparently it's not, since YOU can be modified completely if your brain is modified, even shut off!

I know, I know, God works in mysterious ways.

Why her?

Once in France there was a woman in her thirties who lived as a devout Catholic. She was a math teacher and devoted her free time to helping poor people through a group called *Secours Catholique* (Catholic Help). When I was 16 and I ran away from home for the first time, she and her husband found me. I was sleeping on a tennis court where a friend worked. They took me home. She was not even a friend of my parents. She had gone to school with my uncle. Later in life she stopped working as a teacher and became involved in a retirement home that had been started by her father-in-law, a doctor. As he was aging and unable to keep the business, it faced the prospect of being sold. She and her husband didn't want to see the old folks end up with a for-profit new owner. She decided to take over the reins of the business. These two people lived all their adult lives doing good for others as devout, sincere Christians. At the age of 59, as she was still managing the retirement home, she was stricken by an advanced form of Alzheimer's. Today she can't function by herself and can't live in her house alone.

Why?

I would understand with no problem if only pure, raw, unforgiving biology was involved. She's a multicellular organism, a mammal, a primate and she just got a disease. There is nothing that doesn't make sense if I take the biological realm as a base. But how does this make sense if there is a loving God watching over us? Why do that to someone who lived an exemplary life according to Christian values? Oh, but it's to "test her faith!" Bullshit! Her mind will be gone soon and she won't be able to bother with whether or not she believes in a God. "Oh, but it's to test her devout husband!" Really! So God would sacrifice a human being, a beloved wife, to test a man who all his life believed in Him? What if the husband stops believing? He doesn't go to heaven anymore? What's the point?

What's wrong with your Heavenly Father? You're going to give it to me again, aren't you? "God works in mysterious ways!" Here's yet another case we can't figure out.

Even when parents and teachers test and punish children, we always manage to convey *why* they are being punished, or there's no point. What are we to God that he doesn't even tell us why he does things to us? He doesn't behave as if we were his children, made in his image.

He treats us like cattle.

Faith

Faith is a cop-out. It is intellectual bankruptcy. If the only way you can accept an assertion is by faith, then you are conceding that it can't be taken on its own merits.

Dan Barker

So here we are talking, and suddenly you feel uncomfortable with my arguments and you retreat behind your favorite barricade. Faith. You have faith. I don't. It's a matter of faith, you keep saying. You say that I don't believe because I don't have faith. I always end up asking, "What is faith?" And you invariably tell me, "Well, it's when you believe!" "Ah", I say, "so why do you believe?" "Well, because we have faith - that's why we believe and you don't!" Which comes first, the chicken or the egg? Believing or faith? It's a never-ending circle. Faith, faith, faith! You will use it each time you want to stop the discussion. There is nothing admirable or noble in the act of believing in God and in having faith. On the contrary. At the origin of faith you'll find nothing more than ignorance with a hefty dose of intellectual laziness and fear. Look at the definitions of faith and superstition according to Webster:

Faith: *a firm belief in something for which there is no proof.*

Superstition: *1. a.belief or practice resulting from ignorance, fear of the unknown, trust in magic or chance, or a false conception of causation. b.an irrational abject attitude of mind toward the supernatural, nature, or God resulting from superstition.*

2. a notion maintained despite evidence to the contrary.

Do you see any difference between the two? I don't. Faith is just an excuse for the shutting down of the intellect when the mind can't find arguments or is scared. At some point, intelligence has to say there is no reason to believe in a God. But you want to believe. You need to believe. So what do you do? You simply decide to start apprehending reality and the world around you with something other than your intellect, since obviously your intellect leads you to a place you don't like, a place where there's No God! That's all. That's what faith is. It is something that takes you to a place you deeply want to go but where intelligence can't take you.

Faith is pointless and has never accomplished anything. You owe everything to the human intellect. Look at what brainpower has accomplished in the last 200 years alone! Why should we refuse to use brainpower to tackle any question, including the existence of God? Without intelligent thoughts there would be no electricity, no MRI, no chemotherapy, no antibiotics, no medicine at all. We would all die in our 40s just like in the Middle Ages! Actually without brainpower, our ancestors would never have survived the lions and we wouldn't be here today! The honest, curious, inquisitive human looks at the universe and asks: "Where am I? What's out there?" "Let's search and find out!" She starts looking and searching. She's going to use the tools she has. Her brain and its child, science. Sometimes she's not sure of what she's going to find or even what she's looking for but she keeps searching and testing and thinking until she finds answers. And when she finds no answers, she simply says: "I don't know! I simply don't know! Today I don't know. Maybe tomorrow I'll know." She doesn't allow herself to "invent" stories and theories that suit and please her. Little kids do that. The intellectually dishonest person, the one who is puffed up with faith, has a completely different itinerary. He doesn't ask: "Where am I? What's out there?" And he doesn't say, "Let's look and search!" Instead he says: "I know exactly what I want: I want a God that gives me Eternal Life." So let's build a path that leads to what I want, not what's out there! This is the world and reality built according to wishful thinking! Faith. It's "beyond" brainpower, they say. It's of a more ethereal and spiritual nature, they say. You can't explain what it is. You either have it or you don't. If you don't, well, too bad, you don't "feel" God like the rest of us!

By deciding to ignore human intelligence and shutting down your own, you are actually scrapping all human knowledge. In essence, you decide to tell everybody who has a PhD in astrophysics, biochemistry, embryology and oncology to go tell it on the mountain. You actually have the astronomical gall to tell them they've been using the wrong tools to understand the universe. But you, YOU, have the right one: Faith!

Besides being extremely arrogant and ridiculous, your faith makes you belong to the infancy of the human species, to a time when we had nothing! To a time when we understood nothing! Thunder used to be God shouting his anger at us and he used lightning to punish us.

Praying

If you talk to God, you are praying; if God talks to you, you have schizophrenia.

        Thomas Szasz (professor of psychiatry)

When did I realize I was God? Well, I was praying and I suddenly realized that I was talking to myself.

        Peter Barnes, *The Ruling Class*

Do we have any proof that praying actually works? If it's true that God is omnipotent, all-knowing and all-present, what's the point of praying? Shouldn't He already know what you most urgently need and want? Or is He the kind who needs to be begged and implored? Have you noticed what people pray for? Look at the ridiculous spectacle of a football team praying to win? God cares about football? The creator of billions of galaxies cares about football? If God didn't intervene when the Christians were playing the lions in the Romans' arenas, he's not going to give a hoot about the Steelers and the Green Bay Packers. As I write this, there are people praying in the Congo. They are praying that a group of militants don't enter their village, kill all the men and rape the women, including 5 year old girls. Some of them have screamed prayers to the heavens that some man entering their village would not introduce the barrel of his rifle into their wife's vagina and fire it. That's right! It's a form of torture that has been reported to have occurred repeatedly very recently in the Congo. It was reported personally to Hillary Clinton when she traveled there as Secretary of State in 2009. Many Congolese prayed so it wouldn't keep happening, but God didn't judge it necessary to intervene and stop the horror.

If God doesn't answer that kind of prayer, what kind of prayer is he going to answer?

Feeling God

Truth is an elusive critter, but there is an external reality that science looks at, and if we ignore the objective reality outside of us, we are somewhere between autistic, ignorant, and psychotic.

Michael Hoyt

When Christians and other believers are cornered by anyone telling them they have absolutely no evidence for the existence of God and when they are intellectually trapped by powerful and persuasive arguments of reason and science, they will tell you that you are actually using the wrong tool to "know" God. You must not use your intelligence to "know" God. Instead you should "feel" him, deep in your heart, or wherever it is that you feel things and beings, including God.

What can you tell a Christian who tells you she "feels God?" First have that person agree that God, whom she believes created the Universe with all its billions and billions of galaxies and all the atoms in them, must be infinitely complex. In fact the complexity of an entity capable of creating billions of galaxies and Life itself must be overwhelming. It should not be too hard to have any believer agree with you that God is indeed the most complex entity, thing, essence in the Universe. At least we can all agree on that. If there is a supreme originator He/It is infinitely complex.

Believers tell us that they actually "know" God by feeling him. So apparently it's possible to know a very complex concept, actually the most complex concept in the Universe, God, by using feelings.

This is where I have a problem. To feel, to sense, all those verbs describe ways that are not reliable for knowing the nature of many things, certainly not complex things and absolutely not the most complex entity in the universe.

Ask a believer what she thinks water is. Pour a glass and set it before her. Can she know the essence of water by using whatever she uses to know God? You're asking her to tell you what water is actually made of. You want the composition of water. Tell her that she should forget the 200 years of chemistry that our culture has accumulated and that she should use that same faculty that she uses to know the nature of God to know the nature of water. How does she get to H^2O with feelings? Water, which was, according to that believer, created by God, is much less complex than God. So if she can know God with feelings, she should be able to determine the composition of water with feelings. Can she really, by using that mysterious capacity that lets her know God, come to the conclusion that a molecule of water is made of two atoms of hydrogen bonded to one atom of oxygen? It took our species 250,000 years from the advent of Homo sapiens to around the year 1800 to "know" water when a man named Cavendish found out its composition. Ask your believer friend how long it would take, with that special faculty she uses to know and feel God, to know water. Another million years, another 500 years, half a million years? Try never! She's comparable to somebody who claims to understand the complexity of the human brain, but wouldn't be able, by using the same tool (feelings), to understand anything made by the human brain. That simply doesn't make sense. Today we still don't fully understand the complexity of the human brain, but we can understand anything that it has created. If you don't personally know, you will find in your culture somebody who understands how a car or a computer or a rocket works. Basically the Christian is doing the opposite. They understand, they "know" the engineer, but they don't have the tools to understand the car the engineer built. We humans simply can't "know" the world with our feelings. They are not reliable. Any attempt to "feel" the world, instead of studying it with your brain will produce the wrong result. By consequence, any attempt to know something way more complex than the world, such as the creator of the world, can only be doomed. Any result will be an illusion. A fairy tale. A world populated with djinns and fairies. Look at cultures which are entirely relying on faith and feelings to "know" the world. Afghanistan is one of them. Do they understand matter? Does their culture feel that electricity is electrons moving around? Look at the world that religious fanatics would love to build. It is a world in which nobody knows and where everybody feels. Would you live there? Even the most basic things we take for granted can't possibly be known with feelings. Imagine somebody 1000 years ago, a Native American dwelling on the great plains of the mid-west, or a person living in Siberia going into a big open space where you can see far to the horizon without any obstacles in all directions. If that person is asked a very simple question such as "do you *feel* like the earth is flat or round?" What do you think his feeling will guide him to say? You know very well that he'll put his life on the line to defend the notion that the earth is flat. Your feeling will always tell you that the earth is flat. The feeling of that same person would have told him that each morning the sun rises and moves across the sky and disappears on the other side. It really *feels* like the sun is moving around the earth. Does it, really? It's only through observations and deduction coupled to brain power that we deduced that the earth was actually round. It probably first happened when people realized that the hull of a ship disappeared at the horizon while the mast was still visible. That indicated a curvature of the earth. This is not feelings at work anymore. This is intelligence interpreting observations. Quantum physics, which is the study of matter at the particle level, is totally counter intuitive and nothing in it can be approached with feelings. In this infinitely small world studied by this particular branch of physics, matter and particles behave in very strange ways; so strange that the rules and laws of the physics we're used to don't apply anymore. All the mathematical rules devised

Feeling God

by Newton to study and comprehend the visible world don't apply in quantum physics. In order to study how particles behave, mathematicians and physicists had to invent a new branch of mathematics to comprehend this new reality. So when believers tell us that the creator of water and of our planet (who is infinitely more complex than anything we already can't comprehend with feelings) can actually be known by us with feelings we are indeed entitled to wonder about the validity of their claim. What is it that they are feeling exactly? Could they possibly be fooling themselves? If you do ask them you will be confronted with the following reactions. Some will stop talking to you. They will tell you that they just *know* – that they don't have to be put on the defensive. What a terrible thing it is to have to actually defend your position. Really! Being on the defensive is an attribute of all living things. All earthly organisms are constantly on the defensive, in many ways. Living things are alive and kicking because they are on the defensive. When believers tell you that they don't want to be put on the defensive, they're actually telling you they're dead. Brain dead. Dead wood. Locked forever in rigid ways of thinking, or should I say non-thinking. Certainly not open-minded to new ways. This is the characteristic of scared people always living in fear - constantly afraid of the unknown and of change. They will induce self paralysis to be sure that nothing disturbs them. Of course, as soon as they get cancer, they will rush to science to get those MRI scans. Keep pressing them to describe the feeling that allows them to know that God is real and they will lose patience. You will be cast as evil if you don't believe in him. How dare you ask us to explain anything! All they'll keep saying is "I feel God! I'm sorry you don't! I simply can't help you if you don't feel Him. I really feel sorry for you!"

Let's get the picture straight here. The believer is convinced that you, (the one using your brain, that big brain that has raised the human species above a condition of simple bestiality), that _you_ are the one missing something. He doesn't know what, because he can't tell you how he feels, can't or won't even attempt to vocalize how he "knows" God, but trust him, you are missing it. Some will tell you that you are simply not equipped to feel God and probably never will. Isn't that a gem!? Being inquisitive and trying to use your brain power doesn't actually make you intelligent! It makes you ill-equipped (read "unworthy"). You simply resort to using your brain because you are actually missing a faculty that they have, the one that allows the knowing of God. They will pray for you so one day you too can Know, can *Feel* God with your heart, a muscle in your chest cavity that pumps blood throughout your body.

The New Believer

There's a new breed of believer out there who has upended the relationship between humans and God from what it was supposed to be, according to most sacred scriptures and religious creeds. Until recently, in most segments of Christianity and still today in most of the world, humans were supposed to serve God and follow His rules. People must do what pleases God. In America I'm witnessing the advent of a new kind of believer. This new believer has modified the covenant between God and men. For these new believers God is now supposed to serve them - to pay great attention to their personal situations. God is asked and is actually believed to work daily to make these people's lives better. In the old traditions of Christianity, Islam and Judaism, God imposed rules on humans who had to follow them. Never was God supposed to in fact make life better for mankind on earth.

Quite the contrary. Life is supposed to be a succession of ordeals that determines what kind of afterlife you get. The new believer has reversed the relationship between men and God. Sure, she will do her part to "deserve" heaven, although the constraints have become far looser. The big change is that now God works to make the new believer's life pleasant and agreeable on a daily basis by performing little mini-miracles. Why? Because the new American believer is great! God loves her so much! She's fabulous, worthy, and she deserves to feel good all the time. The new way to believe is pretty much in line with the American way of life. My life will be beautiful, all the time. A never ending party. I'm so special and unique. It's going to be about me, me, me, and if there's any time left, let's refocus on ME! And I'm not going to feel guilty about it because it's actually God's will that I am blessed with all these goodies. The new believer believes that anything pleasant that happens in her day is done because God is watching her constantly and loves her deeply and will go out of his way to make her life great. Why? And why her? Because God loves the new believer like he never loved anybody before. That is what I've witnessed and been told (or made implicitly to understand) by this new breed of even more than usual delusional Christian. If you look at this behavior from a sanity point of view, this is the mother of all ego trips. It reeks of narcissism. Let's put this in perspective; God decided not to do anything for the two children I saw (on a Wikileak video) being fired on when two morons in an Apache helicopter decided to have fun with the 30 mm cannon on their aircraft. God also decides that most suicide bombing missions destined to kill mainly innocent Iraqi or Afghan civilians will be successful. As I write this 59 civilians were killed today by one of those human bombs and miners in Chile are entering their third month stuck in a mine. God will not help Haiti. Totally out of the question! But God is working daily to make the lives of many of these new American believers better with simple things, little details, so our new believer will have a wonderful day? Actually today our new believer had a good day driving to work because God provided for light traffic? Today she was good with her food and didn't pig out on ice cream because God actually helped her not to want ice cream? God is actually so busy improving the life of this particular middle class American creature that he hasn't been able to give any attention to the more than 3 million kids who are, at the time of this writing, threatened by infectious diseases in Pakistan because of the devastating floods ravaging the country? As far as Secular Humanism is concerned, all relationships with any god are delusional. Still, some relationships can appear noble. In the old Christian tradition many people had the strength not to make any demands for themselves and lived lives focused on serving others and their God. Surely Mother Teresa was arguably the mother of all altruists who wanted only to serve her God and the poorest, sickest people on earth in the slums of Calcutta. Compare her to the new believer who has *God* serve *her* and love *her*. What we see in this new Christian is actually a disease. It's the symptom of somebody who hasn't been able to find a place among humans, in society and in her culture. When I look at the lives of this new breed of delusional believer I've always been able to see that most of these people fall into two very broad categories. Either they have had everything or they have had nothing (or at least think they have nothing). The ones who've gotten everything they wanted (and we can count among them some successful millionaire businessmen, politicians and Hollywood actors) subconsciously harbor a strong measure of guilt about having so many riches and such an easy life. They rationalize what they have by simply chalking it up to "God's will." God loves me and wants me to have good stuff. The others are at the opposite end of the spectrum of success in society. They believe they have nothing and certainly are not where they want to be in life. Those I know personally belong to the second category and have failed in many areas of their lives. They haven't been able to retain the love of a spouse or partner. They haven't been fulfilled by their profession. One of them even mentioned to me that she was an impostor, just "playing a role" in her professional life. It turned out that she actually played roles all the time, including in her friendships. They don't live where they want to be living, they don't drive the cars they want to drive. Some have been hit by crippling diseases and illnesses. In all of them I feel some void, some incapacity to really relate and value the world of living humans around them. Everything is about pretending and role playing so they can look good to other humans who they think are watching them. This type of believer is so lonely, so unsatisfied by the real world and what they have been unable to achieve that they come to feel that the only answer for them is to establish a relationship with the only creature they believe will work with them and for them unconditionally; an imaginary God. But where the nun of the past would actually give her life to serve God, the new believer, since she has nothing, wants the opposite. God becomes her servant. Since nobody seems to have loved her, she will end up being loved by God who apparently gets up each morning wondering how He's going to make her life more pleasant. What better revenge, when you feel you've never been loved and cared for by humans, than to be loved and coddled and served by God Himself! Who needs humans after that? The delusion can be pretty extreme. I knew a minister who was twice struck down by the most devastating of diseases, cancer. But he professed to me that these were "acts of love" that his God had actually *sent to him* to make him a better, more decent human being! (I did feel like telling him that he probably didn't have any business being a minister if he wasn't on the high end of decency to start with.) Ironically, that man of God did end up by showing me that he was, after all, still far from being decent and certainly didn't have the makeup of a religious or spiritual leader. In this particular case the terminal disease is not cancer, but serious delusion. What's important to realize is that this behavior doesn't stem from evil intentions. It's the last refuge of those who got nothing out of life. Maybe they failed themselves by setting unrealistic goals? Maybe they were failed by the rest of us in our often harsh society. Can we really blame somebody for seeking refuge in an imaginary world because the real world never provided anything good? "Clinging to religion" as Obama said during his campaign in a totally different context, should not be seen as anything else but an attempt to escape a frustrating, disappointing reality for a better world. In that respect a humanist society, that would value humans independently of their social-economical status, would benefit greatly these individuals.

Why don't they believe?

It was, of course, a lie what you read about my religious convictions, a lie which is being systematically repeated. I do not believe in a personal God and I have never denied this but have expressed it clearly. If something is in me which can be called religious then it is the unbounded admiration for the structure of the world so far as our science can reveal it.

Albert Einstein in *Albert Einstein: The Human Side*, edited by Helen Dukas (Einstein's secretary) and Banesh Hoffman

Who are Humanists and Atheists? Do we find them in the most ignorant, uneducated layers of society, or the opposite? Are they the most courageous, the most stupid, the most altruistic or the most selfish among us? What kind of humans would actually renounce eternal life in heaven in exchange for very small sacrifices? Yes, the sacrifices asked by the Creator to get to heaven are very small. Frankly, the requirements to go to heaven are ridiculously low. Getting to heaven is the easy part of life. Getting into heaven is way easier than getting into med school or law school or any school as a matter of fact. All that's required is to believe in God, not kill anybody, not covet other people's stuff, not steal and not be evil. I'd say that most of us have that covered, so at worse most people will transit momentarily through purgatory en route to heaven. The immense majority of mankind will get to heaven. I'm wondering what happens in purgatory. Do we take remedial classes on how to be really good? Or is it more Taliban style? Are we whipped in some purgatorial public place while the angels in heaven are watching us? Since it is so easy to go to heaven, easier than getting into most human institutions, how come some humans actually refuse the possibility of going there? There is absolutely nothing to lose in living by going to heaven. Still, some humans, who have not and will not kill, covet or steal, have decided they aren't interested. Who are these fools? What kind of irresponsible, frivolous losers are they?

In 1996, *Nature*, one of the world's most prominent and famous scientific journals conducted a survey in which they polled scientists, all of them members of the National Academy of Science (NAS). The following was reported by *Nature* in 1998: "Our survey found near universal rejection of the transcendent by NAS natural scientists. Disbelief in God and immortality among NAS biological scientists was 65.2% and 69.0%, respectively, and among NAS physical scientists it was 79.0% and 76.3%. Most of the rest were agnostics on both issues, with few believers. We found the highest percentage of belief among NAS mathematicians (14.3% in God, 15.0% in immortality).

Biological scientists had the lowest rate of belief (5.5% in God, 7.1% in immortality), with physicists and astronomers slightly higher (7.5% in God, 7.5% in immortality)." Basically the top American scientists have an average rate of atheism averaging 80%. We are dealing with the most brilliant minds alive today whose work has allowed us to probe and know the universe that surrounds us. Their work has allowed mankind to cure diseases, to send men to the moon and bring them back alive. Thanks to them, we know so much about our planet, the oceans, the human body, our brain; everything from our position with respect to other species, to the molecules that keep you from feeling pain when you go to the dentist. Basically this group of people can be called anything but stupid. And no one can claim they have not done their part to improve mankind's lot. What's the message to retain when we contemplate that some of the most intelligent humans, whose work has defined our culture and society, think there's no God, no soul, no heaven? You, the believer, do you have something that Watson and Crick, the discoverers of DNA, don't have? What is it that you know that Einstein didn't know? What have you done, other than believing and going through life powered by wishful thinking and being afraid of death that could give credibility to your position?

Why are you good?

If people are good only because they fear punishment, and hope for reward, then we are a sorry lot indeed.

Albert Einstein

Do you know what really, really gets on my nerves with many believers and particularly with Christians? They are good for the wrong reasons. I've seen it over and over again. Too many Christians are good because they are afraid of what God might have in store for them if they are not. They are not trying to *do* good; they are working at saving their own souls and a spot in that fairytale place called heaven. Can you imagine living like that? Constantly feeling that some higher power has decreed that you must do something, but not really feeling like doing it? Can you imagine the neurosis and the myriad of psychological problems that can arise from such a life?

Who's a more worthy human being? Is it the person who gives a buck to a bum every day because he's counting on God to keep track of this? Or, is it the person who knows that nobody has seen her act of kindness, because it's lost in the universe, there's no reward, but tonight the bum will eat? Generally speaking, do you enjoy the company of people who are motivated by deep self interest? Do you know a bigger motivator than working to get a place in heaven? Is the love or kindness from that person real?

I'm not kidding myself-the person who knows that nobody, including God, saw her give a dollar to that street person, could also be motivated by self interest. It feels good to know that you have made a difference. Still, she didn't have to. She could have chosen to feel good doing many other things. But she chooses, every day, to give a buck to the bedraggled guy who keeps all his belongings in a rusty shopping cart. That giver, whether she feels good or not, is actually capable of empathizing with the situation and the pain of being a bum. The more I look at evangelical Christians, nothing is less sure! When thousands of the survivors from Katrina where trucked into the infamous Dome, Barbara Bush thought it appropriate to point out that, even though the sanitation conditions were appalling, this was "the best those people had had in their lives". She is a devout Christian! Her husband, while in office, even said that atheists are not real Americans. Do you think Barbara felt even a twinge of Louisiana's pain as she watched the drama unfold on her wide screen TV? Do you think she empathizes with the suffering of people who make two or three less zeros on their paychecks?

By requiring people to be good so they can go to heaven, Christianity is building a world of impostors, of fakes. These people are not only just "working" for themselves, but are also removing meaning from what it means to be part of the Human Diaspora. I want a world in which children are taught to empathize humanely with the suffering of others. I want a world in which the innate ability of our species to express altruism can be embraced because it is quite simply the right thing to do to be good to each other. I want a world in which every human being is taught to feel the pain of others and then do something to alleviate it. I don't want a world of selfish intentions in which we are doing good just because it's good for *me* and saving *my* soul and getting *my* ass to heaven.

So you're attracted to that pretty girl or handsome guy?

Have you wondered why you are mainly attracted to, well, people who are attractive? If we are indeed souls who are just temporarily using bodies to go through terrestrial ordeals, set up by God in order to be rewarded with heaven or hell, why does it matter for me to select a mate with nice muscles, long legs, curvaceous hips and other physical attributes that will actually give an edge to the kids we produce? An edge means a biological edge over other humans, my brothers and sisters I'm supposed to love, not to compete with, remember? Having an edge through selecting mates would be relevant if we are only one more animal species among many others and not, according to many so-called sacred texts, as souls incarnated in bodies. In a world according to the Word of God and the Bible, physical fitness should not matter and attractiveness should be largely irrelevant. And yet, we do choose our mates, whether it's for life or for temporary entertainment, according to criteria that have nothing to do with biblical values and more with what survival of the fittest would demand in the animal world. In the case of sexual entertainment, our species has developed the ability to decide consciously to use sexuality for pleasure and not for the purpose of reproduction. Even in that case, when we are not necessarily looking for traits in a partner that would increase the quality of our offspring, we are looking for traits that satisfy the pleasure experienced by our highly elaborate nervous system. It's totally fine with me, nothing wrong with that and I'm all for it, but I fail to see God's design and intention in all this. Certainly not the God the Bible mentions. All over this country Christian men and women are choosing mates, boyfriends, girlfriends, husbands, wives, lovers and mistresses the same way animals are choosing their mates. Why does that girl need to have wide hips? Is that a sign that she can carry babies? What does that girl need to have big breasts? Is that a sign to tell males she can lactate? By the way, why would God allow a female who can't carry babies or lactate to even be born? Why does that male need to be strong and tall? Is that a sign to the female that he can compete with other males? Be a better fighter? Why a better fighter? Aren't we supposed to be living in a world created by a God full of love who has only one goal; to see us love each other? Why did he build us to fight with each other? The only qualities we should be looking for in a mate are the ones valued by the Bible. We should be looking for kindness, generosity, altruism and piety. Instead we look at traits that, when passed to our kids, are going to enable them to crush their playmates. If we were not a mammal species, a primate strongly related to chimps and gorillas, there would be no reason for the human male to be bigger and stronger than the female. The reason why males are stronger and bigger is not because they are the designated meat provider by the species. Lions are bigger than their females, but the females do all the hunting. Gorillas don't hunt and neither do elephants. Still the males are bigger. Why is that? Males in the gorilla, chimpanzee, elephant and lion species are bigger than females for only one reason. To compete against other males of the same species for access to females. Men are bigger than women for the same reason that male lions are bigger than female lions. The larger, stronger male gets to reproduce with the female. That's right boys, God made you bigger than your sister so you could kill your brother competing for your female cousin. And this is the mark of a universe built by love and for love? Human intelligence has added other layers on top of that primitive way to choose mates. Some women just might have a "thing" for artists, or masons or bakers. I'm not trying to pretend that today we are as basic as primates to the point that only physical traits and dominance are considered by humans in choosing a mate. I'm saying, and all evolutionary biologists will back me up, that when we look at the human species we can see where we are coming from. We are coming from a species in which males who were bigger had an evolutionary advantage over smaller males as far as access to females. There is absolutely, and by no stretch of the imagination, any connection between this state of things and the world described in the Bible. Today men don't compete the way their ancestors used to. Nowadays they do it with wealth and status. This is why many women are very sensitive to man's status. Money and power are other ways to be bigger. I don't literally kill you; I buy you out, or should I say, I buy her in! Now from the female point of view. Why do you think some women enjoy watching football? Women who never practiced the sport and who are probably not really interested in its mechanics. Do you think most of them truly care about watching men carry an oblong ball across a field ? Would these women watch *women* playing football? I doubt it. One woman once told me that she actually enjoyed watching "...all those tight asses running around!" The firm derriere signals a powerful musculature and most women are sensitive to that. It signals a fit male. Besides tight butts running around, what could football represent for a female brain? Football is about physically sexually desirable men colliding with each other and getting in situations that resemble fighting. Could it be that for some female brains football produces the same stimulus that was produced when females used to watch males fight among each other for access to them? Could it be that football brings them back, for a moment and completely subconsciously, to that distant past where males had to fight for access to females? There's probably more to it and I assume some women do simply enjoy the athleticism of football. Consider that these same women could watch the buns of 100 meter sprinters, but most of them don't. How come? The clashing, the fighting seems to be a crucial element, and I bet it is. This is simple biology at work here. Of course, explaining everything with biology in today's humans would be an oversimplification, but discarding it altogether would also be a mistake.

Why would a loving compassionate God have built us like that? When I look at my body next to that of a woman, I know that God didn't build me to "biblically" love her or my fellow males. In mammals, males are also bigger to be able to take females by force, if no other males are around. This is inconsistent with the Bible's description of human love, brotherly love.

If we were not animals and clearly God's children put on earth to love each other, many people would be able to fall in love with extremely ugly, handicapped mates who would be kind, generous and loving. Most people do not. Why is that? Instead we want the most beautiful mate with nice breasts that say I'll have milk for your babies, and nice haunches that say, my muscular system is sound, I'll make strong babies for you that will be able to crush the babies of that other female over there! All this makes sense in a world ruled by biology and evolution in which beauty is a marker for good genes.

If I'm not just another primate species, but a soul incarnated in a body waiting to be judged to go to heaven or hell, why does it matter that I choose a mate according to traits that make my species successful?

Can God be mad at you for not believing in Him?

I cannot imagine a God who rewards and punishes the objects of his creation.

Albert Einstein

I've met many Christians in whom I've sensed doubt. Clearly these people are not as fully convinced by their religion as they used to be. Still they keep believing. It has occurred to me that one of the reasons they do is fear. Fear of what God could do to them to punish them for not believing. Does that fear of being punished by God for not believing in him make sense, and is it consistent with the concept of an all-loving God? Remember that God is supposedly omniscient, which means he knows everything, including the future. By consequence He knows everything that will happen to you, including the fact that you might not believe in Him. It's written. He knows it. So don't worry. Before creating you, God already knew He would have to be mad at you because one day you'd stop believing in Him. By the way, how does this make you feel? Do you still feel like a free human being in control of your destiny, or do you feel like a puppet? Still, let's propose some reasons why your God can't be mad at you if you stop believing in Him. One big reason, maybe the biggest of all: what harm does it do the Creator of billions of galaxies and all the matter in the universe that one measly human loses his faith? Can you - the miserable human crawling on the surface of planet earth – actually hurt such a powerful entity by ceasing to believe in Him? Do you honestly think you are important enough that God might be inconvenienced by your loss of belief? I thought not. Which matters the most in the eyes of the God described in the Bible? That you lead a moral life by not killing, not stealing, not making anybody miserable and actually helping other humans or that you believe in Him? What's going to create the most good in your immediate universe and in the universe at large? What if you believe in God and you decide, depending on your faith, to go kill doctors who provide abortions or blow up non-believing infidels with a vest full of explosives in the metro? What do you think God would rather have you do? Believe in Him and kill people in his name, or not believe in Him but spend your life helping the poor and the suffering? Do you believe that the God advertised in the New Testament could be angry at anybody helping the poor? Could He rage against someone who never even thought about

Can God be mad at you for not believing in Him? 137

killing or robbing, who is loving and caring but doesn't believe in Him? Could God hold a grudge against somebody who actually lives like Jesus lived, but who doesn't happen to believe in Him? Do you really believe that your God could punish such a Secular Humanist with hell or even purgatory? What about the Australian aborigines who, until the 19th century (1900 years after Jesus supposedly lived), literally never heard of your God until white colonists forced the gospel down their throats. Is your God going to be angry at them for not believing in Him when they had no knowledge of Him? And today, is He going to be mad at them for viewing the Christian religion as the religion of the white man who oppressed them, stole their land and enslaved them? Could your God full of love and compassion do that? If there is a God, one who supposedly loves us, one so powerful He created all of life, He can't possibly care whether or not I believe in Him. It makes no sense! A God such as that would have no ego – no self-serving cosmic need to be worshiped.

All He would want out of us is decency.

Conversation with a Christian

You can't convince a believer of anything; for their belief is not based on evidence, it's based on a deep seated need to believe.

Carl Sagan

I've asked many Christians and other believers why they believe in God. Each time I have to come to the conclusion that they believe in God for only two reasons - they want to and they can. I have to agree with Carl Sagan referenced above. The mistake most non-believers make is to approach believers with arguments. We try to discuss rationally with them the centerpiece of their belief, God, when it is, of course, a background in psychology that is needed. Believing is a psychological need and you cannot use science and logic to argue away a need, especially if you are not able to propose a faith-based alternative or something else that can provide as much comfort. If you remove what satisfies such a deep-seated need without finding a replacement, all that's left is a vacuum and a collapse of the mind and eventually of the person. The need for a God is not an intellectual need. It is visceral and managed by emotions, fears and desires, not by reflection and critical thinking. Believers don't say, "What's out there? I'm curious. Let's find out!" Instead they say, "This is what I want - a loving God who forgives my mistakes and gives me eternal life! How do I get there?" It's basically the opposite of empirically based modern thought developed in western culture over the last 200 years with the scientific method as its cornerstone. Religious believers behave very much like people used to behave before humans developed scientific thinking. In some ways they still act like uneducated third world people for whom the world is populated and managed by djinns, spirits and demons. Nowhere in the industrialized world is this irony as prevalent as in America. This is a first world nation that has been propelled to where it is today by the work of an extraordinary thinking minority. But the bulk of the citizenry is very much like that of a third world nation. It is an amazing fact that we are harboring within our society such a large number of individuals who have not been taught to think in the way that made western culture great. This has been largely the result of an educational system favoring the acquisition of skills and neglecting the development of critical thinking. We are a nation of technicians, whether we are repairing knees, plumbing or planes and not a nation of researchers and philosophers. Those are a minority. Most people are taught *what* to think, but not *how* to think – and certainly not how to question. The conversation which follows is a composite of all the "arguments" I've had the chance (or the pain) to hear while talking to believers in many real conversations. You will note that most of the time, if not always, the believer in this conversation doesn't answer my question. Instead he jumps to another subject with another question or statement. This is not a fluke in my writing. This is really what I have experienced. When believers are cornered and unable to answer they just drop the subject and jump to something else hoping that this time their argument will fare better. It never does.

Why do you believe in God?

Oh come on, you don't really believe that all you see around you just happened with no cause?
Okay, you need a cause. Nothing wrong with that. But why do you allow yourself to adopt a cause just because it "feels good"? A cause that is not the fruit of research and analysis, but instead is fabricated by wishful thinking and by what pleases and suits you? You want eternal life, so your "cause" of the universe is a God that gives you eternal life. How very convenient. Those of us who think, who live through reason are not ashamed to say we don't know for sure the source of the universe. We are not arrogant enough to say that we know absolutely. There is strong scientific evidence for the event called the Big Bang to have happened, but nobody is 100% sure. But you – you know without a shadow of a doubt it was a supernatural being? Who are you? What do you have that we don't? Why so much arrogance? Do you really know, or do you wish very hard you knew? Is it arrogance or delusion?

But life would be meaningless without a God!
Speak for yourself! Maybe your life would be meaningless. I and many other Secular Humanists are doing just fine thank you! Just because you fail to build meaning in your world, in your existence, if it hasn't been created by a God, doesn't mean I fail too. You find meaning in a parallel imaginary universe you cannot prove and in a God you've never seen. I find meaning in my own existence and in the people I love and who love me, in their presence and actions.

But the Bible tells us that there's a God! The Bible is the word of God!
We don't even know who wrote the Bible! The Bible is pure folklore. It's not even historically accurate. The Bible is no more valid than any other "sacred texts" that you regard as irrelevant or blasphemous. I would wager you don't believe in the Koran, the Torah, Buddhist sacred texts or the Tibetan Book of the Dead! I bet you view them as pieces of folklore each specific to a particular culture! A Tibetan monk views the Bible as a piece of folklore too, specific to your culture. The Bible is just the folklore that your culture has chosen.

But if there's no God, why should I be good?
This is the most disheartening and alarming statement. Any intelligent human who intends to live happily in a community and grow old and safe in it knows that she doesn't need any order from God to figure out that the only

way to assure her own safety in the long term is to actually assure that of her fellow humans. Be good to me and I'll be good to you is the basic tenet of all religions. Treatment of the elderly, for example, is an important marker in all cultures. It's actually even more widespread outside the Judeo-Christian tradition. African and Native American traditional societies as well as many indigenous populations respect and care for their elderly much more than we see in cultures sharing the Judeo-Christian tradition. In America, the most Christian of all industrialized nations, older people are not particularly revered or respected. Rather than being central to our culture, they are more often treated as its refuse. Very early humans had to have understood the need to be good to each other – their very existence depended on it. Even today we see the non-respect of this basic behavior as deviant, always punished. This equilibrium is constantly and often disturbed, but nobody has ever questioned its validity. Altruism is in fact practiced by many animals living in groups, from wolves to rodents.

The fact that so many Christians asked me what the incentive would be to be good without a God just reinforces what I always suspected. These people don't live the way they *want* to live. They live the way they think they are *supposed* to live. They are not really "good" people but fake "good" people who are struggling to be good for the wrong reason. I wonder about the kind of neurosis Christians can develop in their lifetime. I would suspect that being "forced" to live in a certain way while you have other desires and envies is probably at the root of many deep psychological problems. In *Good Without God: What a Billion Nonreligious People Do Believe* by Greg Epstein and *Can We Be Good Without God?* by Robert Buckman, we learn that the human species, which is highly social, is naturally wired for altruism. This is biology. Our brain is built this way for survival. Humans didn't make it in the long primal night in Africa as isolated individuals, but as a group, tightly knit. There is no need for a higher supernatural directive for most of us to go about our daily existence without wanting to kill, main, rape and rob. Do you understand why you should stop at the red light? Because if you don't, the other guy will say, "I'm not stopping either" and eventually we all die. No need to refer to some imaginary supernatural being to understand why we are motivated not to hurt each other. Being "bad", or wanting to harm other members of the tribe/group, is a widely occurring genetic variation in human beings and societies have had to cope with this since the beginning. That's why we have laws and punishments and the Ten Commandments. Maybe we do need religion to keep some of us from going postal? Maybe religion is what mankind invented to keep in check the ones among us who couldn't understand why we should be good to each other?

So that's it - you believe that when you die you die, there's nothing else?
Here we go again. Fear. You are scared by what you can't see in the dark, so you seek comfort in a parallel and

imaginary world in which you don't die at the end of the story. We all need our happy ending, but you do go one step too far. You don't like what you have, so you imagine a world you want. Children do that. Do you expect me to respect that?

You can't prove there's no God!
Do you realize all the things that don't exist and that I can't prove don't exist? For example, what if I tell you that at night in your neighborhood there is a unicorn that walks around. And it's not just an ordinary unicorn. It's an invisible unicorn which also levitates so it doesn't leave marks in snow or mud and infrared cameras can't see it. It's also weightless and can't be detected by any instruments made by NASA or MIT. Since I can't see or detect that creature I just can't prove to you that it doesn't exist. Do you really believe there is such a creature walking around at night in your neighborhood? Do you realize the vapidity of the pronouncement that "you can't prove there's no God!?" First of all, the burden of proof lies with the one who says there *is* something. I don't claim the existence of anything, therefore I don't have to prove anything. I don't know what's out there. I have no idea what was before the Big Bang. I don't have to prove to you why I don't know anything. You are the one who says that you know. You're telling me that before the Big Bang there was God. *You* are the one who needs to show *me* proof....and no, the Bible or your grandmother's faith are not proof.

I have faith. You're in the dark. I feel sorry for you. I sincerely hope that one day, maybe, you'll be enlightened like I am.
The ultimate arrogance. You throw down the gauntlet that I don't know God because I'm missing a receptor that allows you to "feel", to "know" God? You have it and I don't. Really? I haven't been too impressed with your "arguments" from the beginning, but now you are joining the ranks of the ludicrous. I'm missing a magic, secret compartment in my body or my mind that you have? This is delusion, pure and simple.

When all else has been exhausted, the believer becomes The Faithful. Faith is the ultimate argument that believers will throw at you when cornered by human reasoning.
And that's usually where it ends. When I reach the point where these people tell me that they have, without question, found the origin of the universe while our best minds are still working at it, I give up. I no longer engage and debate religious believers face to face. This is totally pointless as they are unreachable. If you catch yourself trying to use reason and intellect with one of The Faithful, stop, take a deep breath and just remind yourself what Carl Sagan said. "You can't convince a believer of anything; for their belief is not based on evidence, it's based on a deep seated need to believe." Realize and acknowledge that you do not have the necessary training in psychology and human behavior to provide something based in the real world that could bring the same kind of comfort and happiness that the myth of religion brings them. It is

simply not rational to believe that when you die there is a part in you, (whether you call it the soul, the spirit, or something else) that doesn't die. You will <u>not</u> be able to use reason and intelligence to communicate about this with a believer. You can only influence people when they are on the same wave length of intelligence and rationality. Believing that you are an immortal soul temporarily inhabiting a mortal body is not rational. It belongs to the realm of wishing, uncontrolled emotions and delusion.

Now the funny, hilarious part; people who don't use reason but just believe in what pleases them will be convinced that you, the person who is not powered by wishful thinking or controlled by emotions -*you* are the one who is wrong.

Let me repeat this: People who believe in holy ghosts, in supernatural events and in their immortality forever in Heaven, next to their God, will believe that you, the one using your intelligence and rationality, **_is_** the one who is wrong. This is delusion mixed with fear and extreme psychological powerlessness. Acknowledge that you are not equipped to deal with this. Do yourself a favor. Turn around and walk away.

Why is religion dangerous?

Anyone who engages in the practice of psychotherapy confronts every day the devastation wrought by the teachings of religion.

> Nathaniel Branden, Ph.D., Psychologist
> author of *The Psychology of Self-esteem*

The greatest horrors of our world, from the executions in Iran to the brutalities of the IRA, are committed by people who are totally sincere.

> John Mortimer, quoted in *The Observer*

I've been told many times to let it go. So what if people believe that they are the creation of a God who will reward them with eternal life after they die. What's the big deal? Why can't I just accept differences and accept that some people believe? Even though dangerous behavior generated by religion is something most people will not have to deal with, it's worth remembering that some religious people in America believed they were told by their god to kill doctors who provide abortions, to drag black men behind pick-up trucks, to kill gay people and to start wars. In his book *Bush at War*, Bob Woodward reports these quotes: "To answer these attacks and rid the world of evil," says Bush, "we will export death and violence to the four corners of the earth in defense of this great nation." Woodward comments, "The president was casting his mission and that of the country in the grand vision of God's Master Plan." The behavior of such an American President, as well as that of somebody who decides to murder an abortion provider, or a Muslim who decides to blow himself up to kill "infidels", are not the norm. Most people will not have to deal with such radical views. Instead of facing extreme and violent behavior, most of which aim directly or indirectly at ending somebody's life, most of us in this country are faced with more tame expressions of faith. Still, despite not being extreme, this behavior seriously detracts from our daily human experiences, removing us from our humanity and its meaning.

I used to know a woman who is a devout believer. Everything that happens to her, or in life in general, is "God's will." She applies this even to actions of empathy and aid from her fellow humans. When I met this woman she had just had a total hip replacement. Just 6 months after her operation she could not do any hard physical work. So one day we decided that I would help her do some yard work. She needed my help to lay down stones in her front yard that she simply couldn't lift. After all the hard, sweaty work was done, all the stones laid down the way she wanted them, I sat down, a little tired, on her front porch. I felt good to have helped a woman I was really starting to like and whose company I was enjoying. I had taken time away from editing a film I had produced and I considered my work as a meaningful gift. I almost passed out when she sat down next to me, looked at the yard and simply and calmly said "Thank you God, for this beautiful yard!" I couldn't believe it. I felt like saying "Are you kidding me! Did you see God busting his ass moving stones in your yard? Lady, I did the work! God, as usual, did nothing!" That was the beginning or our relationship and I decided to remain silent and see if I would see another occurrence of this particular behavior. Unfortunately I did, again and again. Basically she believed God had sent me to help her and it was He who deserved her gratitude. My kindness, my taking time away from my project, all that was actually dismissed. I was not really showing kindness to her. I was just a tool that God had put on her path to make her life easier. I felt negated in my humanity. Later that summer, when I suggested that she should actually buy some exercise equipment, she found used dumbbells for sale on Craig's List. She told me that the price of the equipment was too expensive; she could only afford half of what the seller wanted. I responded that I was also looking to buy some equipment. Maybe we could buy it together. I'd use it too from time to time. The truth was I had access to gym equipment. I didn't really need anything. I had decided to help her buy the equipment because I knew she really needed it. I listened in disbelief as she told me how she had thanked God for providing a solution when she asked for one by "making" me want to share the cost of the equipment so she could buy the exercise set. Here it was. I had actually been told by God, subconsciously of course, to help her split the cost of the equipment! I didn't really help her. God did ...through me. Eventually I realized that her belief in God made her totally delusional and was going to be a serious hindrance to our relationship, which eventually fell apart. This type of behavior is something I and other Humanists see in many followers of a new type of Christianity, uniquely American for now, and in traditional Islam. The human person is negated and reduced to a tool used by God to accomplish whatever they think God wants to see done. Kindness, compassion and empathy suddenly don't come from other humans. Instead they are just momentary, fleeting states injected by God into certain people so they can follow His plans. After my experience with that particular woman, I started to look more closely at other believers. I did see a weaker form of these same tendencies in many of them. A lot of their actions are not genuine. In most of their actions I find all the sacred preciousness of our present human moments are removed, sacrificed to the bigger vision they think their God has in store for them (and for you and me, by the way). Everything they do, alone, to others, for themselves doesn't belong to them or us or the human collective. It's part of a bigger scheme built by some god. You can see this in the tendency of many Christians, and almost all Muslims, not to want to fight to change what might be wrong in life. This life is just a rehearsal in preparation for the real one that comes in heaven, so why bother. It's God's will. Inch'allah! God's will is going to prevail anyway and He will take care of things. Don't worry, everything will end up being fine. Except that right now, on our planet earth, maybe in their community, things are not so fine. Don't fight pollution or global warming they're part of God's plan and he knows where he's going.

I honestly and sincerely believe that life would be better if the bulk of mankind cherished life on earth for what it is, an amazing, totally gratuitous gift that happened to us for no particular reason. It's up to us to make it ours and beautiful.

The more a country believes in a God, the harsher it makes life for its citizens. Look at the difference between secular Europe and the United States. Today in Europe most people view religion as some cultural manifestation of their past. Most people in France, Spain, and Italy belong to the Catholic Church the way one can belong to a fraternity. There's no real meaning behind it. It's tradition. I saw my father, born in southern Italy in 1941, wear a golden crucifix all his life. Recently he told me that he never believed in God in his adult life. He kept wearing it because it was given to him by his mother when he was born and it was a way to keep something from her literally near his heart. He also joked that it was the only piece of gold jewelry he could wear without raising eyebrows. I found this attitude fairly typical where I lived in southern

Europe. In Northern Europe, where people have amazing social benefits and the best healthcare on the planet, populations have the highest number of atheists of any place on earth. According to Gallup World Polls conducted in 2006, 2007 and 2008, and a study done by Phil Zuckerman, a sociologist from Pitzer College, Scandinavia and Japan have the highest rates of atheists in their populations. The breakdown of atheists per country is as follows: Japan 64%, Sweden 63%, Denmark 62%, Norway 41%. Most other northern European countries are above 35%. Depending on the poll, the population of atheists in the US varies between 3% and 9%. What is worth noting is that Japan and Scandinavia are also the regions where people are the least violent and have organized their society to make life as pleasant and easy and fair as possible. Norway and Sweden, where most people do not believe in God, have amazing safety nets and generous vacation benefits. Maternity leave in Norway lasts 2 years, during which both mother and father can be off, fully paid. In the US, which is the most Christian of all industrialized nations, there is no mandatory paid vacation set by the government (compared to 4-6 weeks required by law in Europe). The US has no mandatory paid maternity leave, no national health care insurance and Social Security stipends are ridiculously low compared to Northern Europe. No other industrialized nation is as violent as the US. The most religious industrialized nation in the world is plagued by crime. It doesn't provide any of the safety nets and social benefits provided by nations whose population is 50%

atheist. In the overwhelmingly religious US we keep executing citizens we believe are guilty of crimes, at the proven risk of executing innocents. However, in Europe the death penalty has been abolished for more than 25 years. In Europe some doctors elect to actually work for free in organizations such as Doctors Without Borders, but I've never heard of any US doctors doing that. If anything, most US doctors seem to be involved in lucrative business or status pursuits. Even though there are other reasons why the US denies to its citizens what millions of Europeans enjoy, it would be a mistake to believe that religiosity has nothing to do with it. When a people is convinced that this life is only a rehearsal and that it's OK to have it hard and suffer to deserve heaven, chances are they might not be inclined to fight for paid vacations, maternity leaves and other social goodies. Perhaps they identify with the Virgin Mary. She didn't have any maternity leave or paid vacations after all! Countries centered on religion such as Iran, Afghanistan, Pakistan, India, Saudi Arabia, Yemen and the US do not seem to value the quality of life of their citizens as much as the more non-religious countries and the wellness of their citizens does not seem to be a priority. Believing in God and in an afterlife in heaven seems to negate any feeling of urgency in this life. Why fix things? Everything is God's will! There's nothing we can do about our problems. All we have to do is work with what we have and be patient. One day we'll die and we'll be all set. Pay attention to the believers around you and you will see this in their "If God wants it" and "If God wills it." Religious thinking has contaminated and permeated all areas of life in the US.

Outside the frame of worship one of the most prevalent ways religious thinking can negatively affect people, in secular life, is through the 12 step program. It started with Alcoholics Anonymous but today you can find a 12 step program for any kind of addiction; narcotics, sex, food etc. For some people, I suspect that attending the meetings can be church-like, practically a substitute. I was briefly friend with a man who used to attend Over-eaters Anonymous. When he mentioned it, I didn't really make anything of it. I had heard about the 12 step programs for alcoholism and I always thought they were just practical steps aimed at helping people. Later in our friendship, which didn't last too long, I had to deal with the fact that he prided himself on going through life without critical thinking. He was actually proud of his anti-intellectualism. I remember him saying about my wife, a university professor, "When I watch your wife trying to intellectualize everything, I smile. I know better. You don't go through life thinking." I've always wondered if he thought the oncologists who saved his life twice were morons, and if the other medical specialists who put an artificial knee in his body were able to do that because they were going through life without thinking. Before fully deciding and facing the fact that he was indeed a total nut job, I did all I could to understand him and salvage our friendship. That's why I decided to attend some of these meetings (in a different location from his) to see what was being fed to him. What I discovered was truly disturbing. I introduced myself as a new member with an eating problem (yes, I lied for the sake of science). At my first meeting an amazing downward spiral into nonsense, incoherence, and religious mumbo-jumbo began. I can't imagine the damage that could have been done if I hadn't been an impostor with a clear mind. Anybody who's even somewhat religious and has no serious inclination for critical thinking and enters these programs is setting himself up to become a slave to the religiosity of the 12 steps. Rebelling later unfortunately is not an easy task. I did pretend to acknowledge that I was powerless over certain types of food to be accepted. I happen to actually believe that people who are addicted to a substance, whether it's nicotine, heroin, alcohol or food *are* powerless. The difference is that my definition of powerless and theirs is quite different. Addictions, all addictions, are a matter of brain chemistry. In the 21st century, answers to various addictions must be and are being found in fields such as neuropsychology and biochemistry. At the end of the day, it's all a matter of chemistry. But the 12 step programs are *entirely* based on religious belief and "handing your will over to God." There are no medical professionals, no workshops with specialists in the field to help addicts. It's all about throwing everything in God's lap! And if you don't believe or doubt God, you're cooked. Despite AA's claim that they do not require that you believe in anything, half the 12 steps instruct you to deal with God and if you are a non-believer, they suggest that you actually *invent* something to be your "higher power!" The meetings are filled with religious prayers and readings and personal tributes to the "higher power". Of course this dynamic of the "powerful" making decisions for the weak is one that exists between captors and prisoners and between tyrannical parents and abused children. All this is pretty much in line with the worst of Christian ideology that claims that we humans are miserable, powerless creatures that should spend our existence crawling at the feet of God, endlessly asking for forgiveness, acknowledging how miserable and weak we are, and how good he is to love us despite our weaknesses. Acknowledge you are powerless is their motto!

In the world I've built for myself, with the help of other humans, I find meaning in what I do and in what other humans do. I decide what meaning is, so I am not powerless. Because I'm lucky to live in an industrialized country, and have an education, I can decide how I will give meaning to my life. I am not powerless. I can change things through my own efforts. If anything, I would be powerless if I had remained the way some people think a God made me. He put me naked and defenseless on this planet surrounded by carnivorous beasts and left me to do everything myself. I, as Human, fix my own body when it fails me because my scientific study has allowed me to understand how it works. I arrived where I am today by my efforts only. I made the glasses that allow me to see when the eyes He gave me fail. I made the prosthesis that allows me to walk after my leg is blown off by a religious fanatic armed to the teeth for God. I managed to find a way to live healthily into old age, instead of dying young as he had me do for most of my existence on this planet. When I don't die of cancer anymore, as I used to, and when I get an artificial knee that allows me to enjoy hiking for many more years, it's not because of Him, but because of my hard work and my thinking. Look where I was 100,000 years ago and where I am now! I am not powerless. I understand brain chemistry and what addiction is because I discovered how molecules work. My Heavenly Father never told me anything. Everything I have, even if it's not a lot, I have because of my hard work. I am not powerless. If one day I find a way not do die anymore it will be thanks to my hard work, again. No thanks to Him. Contrary to what God-fearing people mindlessly swallow, I need *not* die to reap the rewards of a good life well lived. I don't even wish for heaven. I leave that to those who like fairy tales. All I need is to be happy with other humans and make life better on earth, now!

On August 23, 2010 we can read in *The New York Times*: "A federal district judge on Monday blocked President Obama's 2009 executive order that expanded embryonic stem cell research, saying it violated a ban on federal money being used to destroy embryos." As reported in the same article in *The New York Times* we read: "Ron Stoddart, executive director of Nightlight Christian Adoptions, an agency that was one of the original plaintiffs in the lawsuit that led to the ruling, said he was pleased with the judge's ruling." I strongly believe Mr. Stoddart is ignorant and superstitious. Ignorant because he hasn't bothered to get the education that would have told him that an embryo is no more a human being than the genetic material that comprises sperm cells and ovules. Why not have a court ruling about all the sperm that goes down the drain when the sheets get washed. Or the eggs that end their viability on millions of sanitary pads. What makes us human is our brain. I've seen the misguided signs from demonstrating pro-lifers "abortion stops a beating heart." All they do by displaying such signs is to actually display their ignorance about life and the human body. The heart is a pump that circulates blood in the body. It does not think or feel. Ants and cockroaches have hearts. What they don't have is a cortex and certainly not a pre-frontal cortex, which is hugely developed in humans. It is in the cortex that thoughts, emotions and consciousness originate. Who you *are* is happening in your cortex. Your identity is certainly there, not in a pump that circulates blood. Embryos have hearts but they don't have a cortex. Embryos are what we are during the first three months of pregnancy. After that we become fetuses. Fetuses develop the structures that are at the origin of thoughts, feeling, identity and consciousness. This does not occur before week 20 and the structure is not fully functional until the 30th week. There has never been a question of destroying 20 or 30 week old fetuses to harvest stem cells. (By the way, at that stage the embryonic stem cells have already differentiated and are not as available as in early stages.) At the oldest, embryos used for stem cell harvesting are at 12 weeks. At that age we are

Why is religion dangerous?

not dealing with a human being, if you consider that what makes us human is our brain. Some misguided, ignorant, almost universally religious people want us to "spare the life" of a bunch of cells that have no consciousness of themselves or the world, no feeling, no nothing - rather than being able to use those cells to find cures for creatures called humans who have mothers, sons, daughters, hopes, dreams, lives. They are essentially saying that a blob which "could become human" one day has more value than what is already human. Why? Why does an embryo (who, if we are honest, statistically has the potential to become anything, a genius but also a serial murderer or another Hitler) have more value than an already human mother working hard to feed her family or somebody suffering the progressive ravages of Parkinson's disease (one of the most hopeful beneficiaries of stem cell research)? Nobody remembers being an embryo or suffering while an embryo. Not a single human ever remembered being an embryo and for one good reason. The structure that gives a born human its memories and its identity, the outer layer of the cortex, doesn't exist in an embryo. It's not a crime to destroy something that is not yet a human and doesn't have a consciousness in order to save a living human. People who pretend the opposite have an agenda. A religious one. Mr. Stoddart believes that something called a soul enters an embryo while it's still in the uterus or the test tube. Like all other believers Mr. Stoddart has never seen or been in contact with a soul. He actually can't even detect his, but he just magically believes that a soul is some immaterial force that flies (swims?) into an embryo in its development stage. Souls, of course, are "sent by God." So basically, today in the 21st century we have to stop doing critical life-saving research because some individuals believe that some…indefinable, vaporous non-entity has been placed in embryos by some god. Of course, they keep repeating that their God is omniscient (he supposedly knows everything); so the question is why did their stupid God put a soul in a frozen ball of cells that was in some scientist's fridge and that God knew ('cause He's all-knowing) was going to be used to harvest stem cells? God does work in mysterious ways.

It's a crutch, it's a crutch, it's a crutch!

The fact that a believer is happier than a skeptic is no more to the point than the fact that a drunken man is happier than a sober one.

George Bernard Shaw

If I could have had the pleasure to meet Shaw I would have asked him if he was indeed convinced that believers are happier. I'm not convinced at all. Most of them seem confused, frustrated and horribly conflicted. Yes, religion is a crutch and a very primitive one. It hobbles the human mind and causes people to limp through life. It's time for a lot of people to grow up in the world of strong adults who know they're going to die and maintain some dignity in the face of that daunting fact instead of searching for false comfort in some self indulgent theory that promotes the fabrication of "eternal life." You don't have your mommy anymore into whose shoulder you can bury your face when the bully beats the crap out of you. Please, resist the temptation to have another, bigger mommy, a god, a big father with whom you delude yourself. Find the shoulder of another human. It's not that bad. Toughen up!

I know, when you see all the suffering, all the starving, all the maiming that goes unpunished, it's tough to just believe that you're alone, that that's it, that there's no superior power taking care of all that mess. Nobody is seeing or watching. Nobody will be judged and nobody will be punished, except by their fellow humans. Totally unacceptable, I agree, but it's called life on planet earth and it's all we have. As much as you'd love to have a supreme God in charge, watching all this horror and nodding wisely and assuring you the bad guys will pay, it's just wishful thinking. How many hundreds of generations of humans have passed by on this planet, getting old, losing their physical strength, unable to punish or avenge crimes against their brothers, against humanity, hoping that some superior being up there would do it for them… eventually…at the end? It's forgivable, it's human thinking, but it's still wishful thinking. Just as little children grow up and learn the truth about the existence of the tooth fairy, the human race needs to mature and learn the truth about the existence of God. It's a crutch. God is a crutch used by most men and women to avoid panicking about death while they're alive. A god promising eternal life is what all cultures found as the best opiate. The universal comfort. And since mankind at its dawn needed an explanation for the existence of the world, since we didn't have any of the tools of discovery and explanation we have today, we killed two cosmic birds with one stone. We imagined a God that gives us Eternal Life *and* created the Universe.

Please come back!

I'm very disappointed. One more time you've left me standing naked on this planet all by myself. The heat was turned up and once again you ran toward your god like a little kid to his mother. And I'm alone facing the adversity of being a human, all by myself. When life becomes tough, all I have is the strength I find in myself and in the people who love me or who say they do, because so many of you are cheating. When life gets difficult, really difficult, instead of cooperating and trying to reach out to see if we can work out real solutions together, you seek refuge in your imaginary god. You can't take the heat in the human kitchen, so you run scared and crying into God's bedroom! Am I getting this right? You're not going to work with me to fix this world because it's just a rehearsal, just preparation for the "real" reality that will come after you die? It takes courage to be human. It takes courage to accept that you're a mortal living being. It takes courage to see your loved ones get sick, get killed, or die! It's tough to look at your baby born with a deformity. It's tough to see your own body degenerate year after year. Well, guess what? It sucks. But I could take all this if you'd care for me and with me, if you'd fight alongside me and stand by me.

I could take all this if we were a big family, all together, making life on this planet easier for each other. I could take all this if we were precious to each other. You are to me. Most of humanity is to me. I'm not to you because I don't believe in God. Sometime I think that, at best, I'm some kind of ordeal, a tool that your god put in your way so you could experience "challenges" that prepare you for your other world where you're going to be rewarded and live happily forever. Please gather yourself together and come back. Let's give meaning to this mess together. Let's make the mess beautiful, not because a god had decided everything for us, but because *we* have. We can make this world work together. We can find answers and meaning in each other. You don't need that supernatural creature. I'll value you and you'll find me worthy. Don't you see that if we are the way we are for no divine reason, but just because of natural evolution, it gives us the chance to fully belong to ourselves and fully give to others. It makes us much more special than if a god had put us here to be able to punish or reward us – in effect to use us for his own ends? Let's find meaning in us. Not as some supernatural creature's creatures.

Please, come back!

www.ingramcontent.com/pod-product-compliance
Lightning Source LLC
Chambersburg PA
CBHW031352040426
42444CB00005B/264